facebook me!

*A Guide to Having Fun with
Your Friends and Promoting Your
Projects on Facebook*

DAVE AWL

Peachpit
Press

Facebook Me! A Guide to Having Fun with Your Friends and Promoting Your Projects on Facebook
Dave Awl

Peachpit Press
1249 Eighth Street
Berkeley, CA 94710
(510) 524-2178
(510) 524-2221 (fax)

Find us on the Web at www.peachpit.com.
To report errors, send a note to errata@peachpit.com.
Peachpit Press is a division of Pearson Education.

Project Editor: Becca Freed
Production Editor: Myrna Vladic
Copy Editor: Elissa Rabellino
Proofreader: Suzie Nasol
Compositor: Dave Awl
Indexer: Valerie Perry
Interior design: Charlene Charles-Will with Danielle Foster
Cover design: Charlene Charles-Will

Notice of liability

The information in this book is distributed on an "As is" basis without warranty. While every precaution has been taken in the preparation of the book, neither the author nor Peachpit shall have any liability to any person or entity with respect to any loss or damage caused or alleged to be caused directly or indirectly by the instructions contained in this book or by the computer software and hardware products described in it.

Trademarks

Facebook is a registered trademark of Facebook, Inc.

Many of the designations used by manufacturers and sellers to distinguish their products are claimed as trademarks. Where those designations appear in this book, and Peachpit was aware of a trademark claim, the designations appear as requested by the owner of the trademark. All other product names and services identified throughout this book are used in editorial fashion only and for the benefit of such companies with no intention of infringement of the trademark. No such use, or the use of any trade name, is intended to convey endorsement or other affiliation with this book.

ISBN-13: 978-0-321-59195-1
ISBN-10: 0-321-59195-X

9 8 7 6 5 4 3 2

Printed and bound in the United States of America

Acknowledgments

I owe my first and best thanks to Becky Morgan, executive managing editor of Peachpit Press, for calling my bluff last spring when I said I thought maybe I could write a book about Facebook—and then patiently and sure-handedly working with me to guide the project from a half-baked list of bullet points into a plan for a real live book.

Thanks are also due to my project editor, Becca Freed, for her valuable insight in helping me figure out the format and the structure of this book; to my copy editor, Elissa Rabellino, and my proofreader, Suzie Nasol, for their sharp eyes, patience, and flexibility; to Myrna Vladic, Charlene Charles-Will, and Danielle Foster for all their help with design and production issues; to Clifford Colby, Sara Todd, and Glenn Bisignani for early help and input; and to Nancy Davis, editor in chief, and Nancy Ruenzel, publisher, of Peachpit Press.

Tremendous gratitude to my fellow Peachpit authors Sharon Steuer and Sandee Cohen, from whom I've learned so much, for their friendship, support, and sage advice. Working with them on several editions of their own books helped me develop the skills and experience necessary to write this one. In a similar vein, thanks to Terri Stone at CreativePro.com for letting me take my first stab at writing about social networking. And a megalithic *go raibh maith agat* to my old friend and collaborator Corbin Collins, for starting me down this road almost a decade ago. Your next pudding drink is on me.

Speaking of friends, this book wouldn't have gotten by without a ton of moral support, and much-needed encouragement, from mine—especially Jim Farruggio, Lisa Buscani, Jorjet Harper, Diana Slickman, John Pierson, lynne Shotola, Danielle Christoffel, Lori Dana, Sandie Stravis, Kevin Spengel, Tim Clue, Lydia Paweski, and Ayun Halliday, as well as Richard Cooper, Chris Bell, Yvonne Studer, and all the members of the Kraken. A special shout-out to my long-lost college pal and new Facebook friend Dan Loughry, for keeping my music library fresh while I wrote this book. And a primary thanks to my dear friends Tracey Bettermann Wetzstein and Kathy Zant for dragging me onto Facebook in the first place. All of you guys are the reason the Accept button was invented.

Thanks to every single person who gave me permission to use their name and photo in this book (even if I didn't manage to fit you in somewhere); to my high school Original Comedy god Matt Solomon for always being ready in a pinch to help me set up a silly screen shot; and to Jill Bernard, Dan Telfer, Robbie Q. Telfer, Pip Lilly, Vee Sonnets, and the Neo-Futurists for the use of performance-related images.

Thanks to AKMA Adam, Jason Schupp, and Amy Gibby and Michael Martin for offline networking assistance, and to Kirsten Bollen and Craig Donato at Oodle.com for an early look at the new Marketplace. And thanks to everyone who gave me input for the applications chapter, especially Jennifer Senft Lucarelli, Shaina Lyn-Waitsman, Yehudit Hannah Cohn, Andy Heaton, Anne Halston Cook, Jeanne Pierson, Sonya Shalnikov, Aimee Krause, Ian Belknap, Tom Doyle, Kristin Amondsen Sassi, and Leanne Fabrycki Ross.

And finally, I'm grateful beyond words for the love and support of my family: my siblings, Jane and Earl, and Stephen and Sarah; my dad, Richard; and most of all, my mom, Charlotte.

Chicago, January 2009

Contents

CHAPTER 7   **Applications and Other Add-Ons   109**

CHAPTER 8   **Photos and Videos   134**

Introduction

Life on Facebook is full of surprises. In fact, I'm still surprised that I'm on Facebook at all, let alone writing a book about it.

I was not an early adopter of Facebook, to put it mildly. The truth is, I had to be dragged clicking and screaming into the ranks of its users. Like you—I'm guessing—I joined Facebook when I got an invite from someone I couldn't say no to. Two such people, in fact, on the same afternoon.

In the fall of 2007, members of my old college speech team had started joining Facebook—a large, far-flung group of people I love and have had difficulty keeping in touch with in the two decades since I graduated from college. But within a month of joining Facebook, I felt like my old friends were back in my life. I knew where they lived and who they were married to or dating, had seen pictures of their kids and animal companions—and through the magic of Facebook's News Feeds and status updates, I knew what they'd done over the weekend, what was making them laugh out loud, and what songs were stuck in their heads on a given morning.

I have many dear friends who want to remember my birthday but can never seem to manage it. Every year, they start preemptively wishing me happy birthday in March or April —"I know it's around here some-where," they e-mail me—when it's actually not until mid-May. But this year, for the first time ever, all of those people wished me happy birthday *on the actual day*, by writing on my Facebook Wall after Facebook kindly informed them that *this* was the day they could never remember.

That's the single best argument I can think of for joining Facebook and checking it daily: the fact that it can help you stay connected with, and bring you closer to, the people you miss and wish were more of a presence in your life.

My goal for this book is to give you strategies for using Facebook intelligently and effectively. It's easy enough to sign up with Facebook and create a profile—but how do you get the most out of your Facebook experience? How do you use it to make fascinating new friends, build new bridges to people you love but have fallen out of touch with, effectively promote your band or your graphic design business or your café, and generally become the rich and famous rock star you were always destined to be?

Well, okay, that last one might be a little beyond the scope of this book. But the rest of it is definitely on the menu.

How to Use This Book

The structure of this book is fairly self-explanatory. It starts by covering the basics—how to set up your profile, how to configure your privacy settings, and so forth; then moves on to explore Facebook's various tools for communicating and interacting; and then wraps up with some more advanced topics like how to promote creative and business projects, and the workplace politics of Facebook.

One caveat: Facebook changes a lot. The folks at Facebook are always tinkering with and fine-tuning its interface. During the time I was working on this book, controls were renamed or moved on an almost daily basis. So by the time this book makes it into your hands, Facebook may have evolved quite a bit from the version I've written about here. Some of the screen shots and specific instructions you see in these pages may not precisely match what you see on your screen when you log in. Some features I talk about may have been renamed, moved, or removed from Facebook altogether. That's one of the occupational hazards of writing a book about a Web site—especially one that changes as continuously as Facebook does.

The best advice I can give you is not to get too hung up on the specifics as you read this book. My goal is to familiarize you with the general way Facebook works and the kinds of tools it offers. The screen shots and instructions presented here are intended as illustrations and exercises to help you figure out the larger principles behind Facebook's various features—how to use its News Feeds, Events, Groups, Pages, photos, videos, links, and so forth creatively and effectively. Once you understand what it's possible for you to do on Facebook, and get the basic hang of the place, you should be able to use the visual cues provided by Facebook's interface itself to figure out how to get from point A to point B, even if point B isn't exactly where it was the last time you looked.

Facebook generally offers multiple ways to do the same thing—so in the interests of space and not publishing a book that weighs more than your refrigerator, I've usually chosen to explain one expeditious method for accomplishing each given task, rather than describing all 17 possible workflows—or in some cases, maybe playflows. (Is that a word? Can I coin it?)

In deference to my subject matter, I will end this introduction with a ceremonial use of the Facebook third person:

"Dave Awl has written you a book about Facebook. He hopes you like it."

COLOPHON

This book was written and laid out entirely on an Apple MacBook (not even a MacBook Pro, for Pete's sake!) using Adobe InDesign CS3. Screen shots were taken using Snapz Pro X. The main fonts were Warnock Pro for body copy, and the Serif and the Sans for headings.

ON THE WEB

Visit DaveAwl.com for news, updates, and features related to this book. And look for the official *Facebook Me!* Group on Facebook, to connect with the author and other readers of this book.

1

The Anatomy of Facebook

Until you actually join Facebook and play with it a little, it can be hard to figure out what's so appealing about it. Some stories in the media make it sound like the hottest hipster fad since the invention of the black turtleneck, while others portray it as a cross between an opium den and a shark-infested lagoon.

So you put off signing up for a while, wondering: What could possess otherwise sane people to sit hunched over their computers all day, posting photos, playing word games, and sending each other virtual vampire bites or pictures of cute animals? What could possibly make a Web site so addictive that its members refer to it as "crackbook"?

To me, the answer is simple: Facebook does a better job of connecting you with your friends, and keeping you in touch with each other, than any invention since Alexander Graham Bell first crank-called Watson.

You can think of Facebook as the online dashboard for your social life: a centralized display that gives you up-to-the minute data on what your friends are up to, what's on their minds, and what they're planning for the weekend.

But there's another level to its appeal, too. In addition to strengthening social connections, Facebook gives you a set of powerful and versatile tools for sharing information and promoting whatever interests or creative projects you may have cooking. In a sense, Facebook is like having your own personal broadcast network.

If you've got a band, a theater company, a book, a coffeehouse, a graphic design business, or anything else you want to promote, this book will tell you how to set up Facebook Groups and Pages to find fans and customers, and use Facebook's promotional features to get the word out to the kinds of people who are most likely to be interested in what you have to offer.

What Can You Do on Facebook?

In upcoming chapters, we'll look at the various ways you can use Facebook:

- Reconnecting with old friends and making brand new ones
- Keeping track of what your friends are saying, thinking, and doing
- Sharing info with friends by posting notes, links, photos, and videos
- Using applications to play games with friends around the world; send each other virtual "gifts"; spread the word about charities and political causes; recommend books, movies, and music; and much more
- Inviting your friends to parties, performances, meetings, and any other kind of get-together you can dream up
- Creating Groups and Pages to connect with others who have similar interests—and spread the word about creative projects and business endeavors

I'll also give you tips and strategies for dealing with common problems and concerns about Facebook:

- How to protect your privacy and enjoy Facebook safely
- How to evaluate friend requests from complete strangers
- How to decide which apps are trustworthy and which ones to give the brush-off
- How to avoid unintentionally spamming, pestering, or annoying the bejabbers out of your Facebook friends
- How to reduce the chances that your Facebook obsession will get you in hot water at work

But for now, let's start at the beginning, with a guided tour of Facebook's most prominent features.

What's an Application?
Facebook applications let you do all kinds of fun things, from playing games to sending offbeat greetings to your friends. Often referred to as "apps" for short, applications are simply programs designed to run on Facebook. See the *Applications and Other Add-Ons* chapter for complete info on Facebook's applications—what they are and how to use them.

TIP: See the *Privacy and Security* chapter for lots of tips and info on how to make your Facebook experience safe and secure.

The Frame

There are three elements that are the same on every page on Facebook, giving you some consistent reference points to steer by: the blue bar, the footer, and the Applications bar. These elements together are referred to as the *frame*.

The Blue Bar

Running across the top of every page on Facebook is a bright blue bar, known cleverly as "the blue bar." It will be your faithful companion for all your journeys in Facebook, more loyal than Tonto, Robin, or even Dr. Bunsen Honeydew's faithful lab assistant, Beaker.

The left side of the blue bar

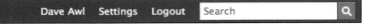

The right side of the blue bar

The links in the blue bar help you navigate your way around Facebook.

- **Facebook** and **Home** take you to your Home page on Facebook.
- **Profile** takes you to your Profile page.
- **Friends** takes you to a page where you can view lists of all your friends on Facebook. If you hover your pointer, a pop-up menu appears with options for finding friends on Facebook and inviting people to join. (See the *Friends* chapter for full coverage.)
- **Inbox** takes you to your Facebook message center. A number next to the word Inbox tells you how many new messages you have waiting (if any).
- On the right side of the blue bar, you'll see **your name**—clicking it will take you to your Profile page.
- **Settings** takes you to your Account Settings page. If you hover your pointer, a pop-up menu will appear that lets you choose the Account Settings page or the Privacy Settings page.
- **Logout** logs you out of Facebook.
- At the far right side of the blue bar is Facebook's **search field**. You can use this to find all sorts of things on Facebook: people, groups, events, pages, and more. You can even use it to search for results on the Web.

TIP: The *Your Name* link on the right side of the blue bar might seem redundant, given that there's already a Profile link over on the left side. But the Name link serves an extra purpose—it lets you know that you're currently logged in as you. If you use a shared computer and you see someone else's name in the blue bar, you'll know they forgot to log out of Facebook, at which point you should log them out and log back in as yourself.

A Brief History of Facebook

Facebook's rise to prominence on the Internet has been meteoric. At the time of this writing, Facebook has more than 100 million members around the world and is still growing by leaps and bounds.

Launched in February 2004 by Mark Zuckerberg, then a student at Harvard University, Facebook took its name from the printed directories known as "face books" that students were given to help match their classmates' names with their faces. The idea behind Facebook the Web site was to build an online, interactive version of a traditional face book, which would allow students to create, personalize, and update their own profiles.

Another important idea behind Facebook was that its members would use their real names, and their identities would be verified by virtue of the fact that their profiles were linked to school-issued e-mail addresses. Unlike MySpace and other popular networking Web sites, no pseudonyms, aliases, or fake names would be allowed on Facebook, thus making its members accountable for how they behaved.

Facebook's membership was originally limited to Harvard, but the site proved so popular there that it was quickly expanded to other universities and colleges, and then high schools, and then workplaces.

The biggest turning point, however, came in September 2006 when Facebook dropped the requirement for a school- or work-issued e-mail account, effectively opening its doors to anyone older than 13 with a working e-mail address. By July 2007, nearly half of Facebook's users were 35 and older, as parents and grandparents joined teenagers and college kids on its rolls. These days, according to Internet marketing research company comScore, Facebook has the most site traffic of any social media site in the world.

Facebook © 2008 English (US) ⬍	About Advertising Developers Terms ▪ Find Friends Privacy Account Help

Facebook's footer

The Language menu

The Footer

Running along the bottom of every Facebook page is a horizontal list of links called the *footer*. It's easy to overlook, but it has some useful resources.

- The pop-up **Language menu** lets you change which language you view Facebook in. (I use this to brush up on my French sometimes.)

- **About** takes you to the About Facebook page, which rounds up press information, hiring announcements, and other company-related info.

- **Advertising** links to information and tools for advertisers. (See the *Pages and Ads* chapter.)

- **Developers** links to resources for creating Facebook applications.

- **Terms** displays Facebook's Terms of Use agreement.

- **Find Friends** takes you to the "Find Your Friends on Facebook" page, which offers a slew of resources for tracking down the people you know on Facebook. (This page is discussed in detail in the *Friends* chapter.)

- **Privacy** gives you handy access to Facebook's privacy policy.

- **Account** takes you to your Account Settings page.

- **Help** links to the Facebook Help Center, which also gives you access to Getting Started tips and Safety information.

The Applications Bar

Down at the very bottom of the Facebook screen is the floating Applications bar, which is always visible regardless of any scrolling you do.

It contains a pop-up menu on the left that gives you quick access to your Facebook applications, and space in the middle to create quick-link buttons for favorite apps. Facebook's Chat application lives in the Applications bar, too, over on the right-hand side. (See the *Communicating on Facebook* chapter for info on Chat.)

The Profile Page

Your Profile page is the page about you on Facebook. It's the place your friends will visit to check out what you've been up to lately, and it's one of the two pages you'll probably spend the most time on (along with your Facebook Home page).

TIP: Who can see the information on your Profile page? By default, only people you've added as friends on Facebook, or people who belong to Networks you've joined. (See the *Friends* chapter for information on Networks, and the *Privacy and Security* chapter for information on how to control who's allowed to view your profile.)

Your Status Update

Up at the top of your Profile page is your *status update*: a one-sentence answer to the question *What are you doing right now?* You can use it to

TIP: Whatever you type for your status update will be visible on your friends' Home pages, and possibly other places around Facebook as well. You can think of it as sending out a little news release to your social circle.

tell your friends what you're working on, what you're eating, where you're planning on going later today, what song is stuck in your head, or anything else that's on your mind.

Dave Awl is working on Chapter 1, and watching the leaves outside his window turn yellow. They get a little yellower every few minutes. 21 hours ago clear

Wall   Info   Photos   Boxes   +

The status update at the top of the Profile page, and the four tabs underneath it

The Four Tabs

By default, your Profile page has four different tabs people can choose to see different kinds of information.

TIP: In addition to the four default tabs on your Profile page, you can add custom tabs for favorite applications as well, using the plus sign menu next to the tabs. See the *Applications and Other Add-Ons* chapter for details.

Wall Tab

The Wall tab is the default view for your Wall. People can drop by your Wall to see what you've been up to on Facebook.

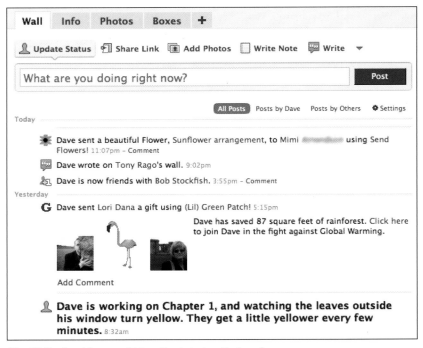

The Wall tab, with several News Feed stories displayed

Your Wall displays short messages, or *News Feed stories*, generated by Facebook to tell your friends what you've been up to lately: who you've made friends with, what Groups you've joined, whose Walls you've written on, and so forth. (These are the same stories that appear in the News Feed area of the Home page, discussed later.) Think of Facebook's News Feed as your own personal PR bureau, keeping your legion of fans up to date on your doings.

People can also post short messages on your Wall (and you can return the favor on theirs).

> **TIP:** By default, messages you write on someone's Wall are public, meaning that other people who visit that person's Profile page will be able to read them. You can think of Wall posts as being kind of like tacking up a note on a neighbor's door, or dedicating a song to someone on the radio.

Today

Dave Awl wrote at 7:48am
Hey Lori, thanks for the Halloween candy! It's a relief not to have to toilet paper your computer ...
Wall-to-Wall

Yesterday

Lori just sent a Halloween Candy to friends. 5:50pm – Comment

Info Tab

When people want to know a little more about who you are and what makes you tick, they click your Info tab. The Info tab rounds up basic data like your hometown, current city, and contact information, plus biographical information (your birthday, where you went to school, and where you've worked) and lists of your favorite music, books, movies, and TV shows.

> **NOTE:** The information on the Info tab is all optional. It's completely up to you what info you want to share, and how much detail you want to go into.

| Wall | Info | Photos | Boxes | + |

Edit Information

Basic Information

Networks: Chicago, IL
              Bradley Alum
              Neo-Futurists
Birthday: May 12

Personal Information

Activities: Writing, performing, dancing, blogging, cleaning the litterbox.
Interests: Tea, cats, mythology, New Wave, old stone circles, skinny ties, sparkly animal pins, Thai food, activism, poetry, nonsense, surrealism.
Favorite Music: The Beatles, David Bowie, The Waterboys, The B-52's, Crowded House, Madness, Lene Lovich, Split Enz, Joan Baez, Mama Cass, Donovan, T.Rex, The Velvet Underground, The Mumps, Patti Smith, Yoko Ono, Joe Jackson, The English Beat, The Bongos, Billy Bragg, The Housemartins, Aztec Camera, Belle & Sebastian, The National, The Kings of Convenience, The Decemberists, The Mountain Goats, Even in Blackouts
Favorite TV Shows: The Kids in the Hall, Doctor Who, House M.D., Mad Men, The West Wing, The Prisoner, Firefly, Arrested Development, The Colbert Report
Favorite Books: Some of my favorite authors: Ursula K. Le Guin, Russell Hoban, Christopher Isherwood, Charles Dickens, James Joyce, Gore Vidal, Paul Monette, Milan Kundera, Kurt Vonnegut, Hermann Hesse, W. H. Auden, Rilke, Yeats, Allen Ginsberg, Frank O'Hara.

Some of the information that can be displayed on the Info tab

NOTE: The Photos tab and the Boxes tab don't appear until they have content to display. So if you haven't posted any photos yet, and none of your friends have posted photos tagged with your name, you won't see a Photos tab on your profile. Similarly, if you haven't chosen to install any applications, you won't see a Boxes tab on your Profile page. But don't worry—both of those tabs will show up once they have a reason to be there.

Photos Tab

Posting and sharing photos is one of the most popular pastimes on Facebook. Once you upload photos to Facebook, you can arrange them into albums and invite your friends to come take a look at them—and maybe even scribble some trenchant remarks down in the comments area at the bottom of the page for each photo.

The Photos tab gives you and your friends quick access to any photos you've posted, as well as photos your friends have posted that include you.

Boxes Tab

The Boxes tab displays a collection of your favorite Facebook applications—the ones you like well enough to "install" so that they appear here.

The Home Page

You can always drop by your friends' individual Profile pages to find out what any specific pal of yours has been up to lately. But your Home page gives you one-stop shopping for news about your friends, including links and photos they've posted, their most recent status updates, and other good stuff.

The News Feed

Right in the center of your Facebook Home page is the News Feed, which rounds up stories about your friends' activities on Facebook (like the ones described earlier in the "Wall" section).

The News Feed has a series of different tabs you can select, in order to see different kinds of stories.

> **TIP:** You can click the triangle menu button on the right side of the tabs for even more options: Filter your News Feed for stories about specific applications, or choose a Friend List to see stories about friends on that list. (See the *Friends* chapter for what Friend Lists are and how to create them.)

Requests

- 3 friend suggestions
- 7 event invitations
- 33 other requests
- 2 friend requests
- 10 sea garden requests

Notifications

- 1 new notification

The Requests area in the right-hand column on the Home page

Applications   Edit

- G (Lil) Green Patch
- Send Good Karma
- Catbook
- Sea Garden
- Pieces of Flair
- SuperPoke!
- ▼ more

The Applications area

Pokes

You were poked by:
- Becca Freed – poke back | remove

The Pokes area

Events and Birthdays   See All

- Friday, October 24 at 9:00pm
  Cake Chicago 2 Year Anniversary Party!
- Friday
  Tracy Brown Collins

The Calendar area

The Right-Hand Column

There are some other goodies on your Facebook Home page, too, in the column on the right side of the page.

- The Requests area shows you a few of the most recent invitations you've received, and links to the main Requests page (discussed in the following section).
- The Applications area gives you quick links to a few of your favorite applications (much like the Applications bar discussed earlier).
- The Pokes area displays any recent Pokes you've been sent. (Pokes are a special kind of "hello" message on Facebook; see the *Communicating on Facebook* chapter for details.)
- The Events and Birthdays area lets you know about upcoming Events you've been invited to, as well as your friends' birthdays.
- And down toward the bottom of the column are some tools for finding people you know on Facebook and inviting other friends to join Facebook. (See the *Friends* chapter.)

Other Kinds of Pages

In addition to your Profile page and Home page, there are a few other places you'll be visiting from time to time on Facebook.

The Requests Page

Clicking any of the links in the Requests box on the Home page takes you to the Requests page, where you can see various kinds of invitations you've received. When other Facebook members invite you to become their friend, the request shows up here. This is also where you'll get invitations to attend Events, join Groups, play games, and interact with your friends using apps.

The Inbox

The Inbox is your Facebook message center—a place where you can send and receive direct, private messages to and from your friends on Facebook. See the *Communicating on Facebook* chapter for more about the Inbox.

The Notifications Page

Notifications are little announcements that tell you something has happened that Facebook (or one of your applications) thinks you should know about.

When someone writes on your Wall, comments on a photo you've posted, accepts your friend request, or sends you a virtual gift, you'll most likely find out about it through a notification.

Your recent notifications are listed in chronological order on the Notifications page, which you can access in a bunch of different ways: by clicking its tab on your main Inbox page, by clicking on any Notification message that shows up on your Home page, or via the handy Notifications pop-up box that lives in the Applications bar, right next to the Chat application.

Groups

Groups are like little clubs on Facebook, where members can talk and post information related to something they have in common. You can create a Facebook Group dedicated to any subject under the sun, and invite people to join it—as long as it's not obscene, hateful, or otherwise in violation of Facebook's Terms of Use.

Events

Events are essentially home pages for calendar events. You can create Event pages for parties, performances, concerts, lectures, movie outings, rallies, or any other kind of gathering, and send out invites to friends you'd like to attend. Facebook allows the invitees to RSVP so you know whether or not they're planning on showing up, and gives you a page on which you and your guests can post information, photos, videos, and other content relevant to the Event in question.

Notes

Notes are short essays you write and post for your Facebook friends to read. You can think of them as blog entries, but instead of being posted to the whole World Wide Web, they're directed to the more intimate audience of your Facebook Friends list.

Facebook Pages

Individual Facebook members are represented by profiles. Public figures and entities like bands, theater companies, TV shows, books, and movies are represented by Pages. A Facebook Page looks like a profile page, but instead of becoming friends with the entity the Page represents, you click a link to "become a fan" of the Page. See the *Pages and Ads* chapter for complete info on how to find, become a fan of, create, and manage Facebook Pages.

> **Notifications**
> 🖵 1 new notification

A Notification message as it appears on the Home page

The pop-up Notifications icon (left) lives next to the icon for Facebook Chat (right). The little balloon with the number changes to tell you how many notifications you currently have waiting for you.

TIP: If you're familiar with Yahoo Groups or Google Groups, then you already have a pretty good idea how Facebook Groups work. And if you or your friends use Evite to send out party invitations, you'll find that Facebook Events work similarly.

Updates from Pages
Once you become a fan of one or more Pages, you may receive *updates*: news and information messages from the bands, TV shows, politicians, and so forth that the Pages belong to. Updates are flagged out in the right-hand column of the Home page and appear on the Updates Page, which you can access by clicking the Updates tab in your Inbox.

2

Signing Up and Setting Up Your Profile

Life on Facebook begins with registering and setting up a personal profile. Your Profile page is where you get to express your personality, your style, your current interests and obsessions. It's the place your friends will drop by to see what's on your mind lately—as well as what's in your MP3 player, your video queue, and your book pile.

Your profile also serves as an introduction to new people you meet on Facebook—it's something like a business card, only with a playful streak, a listing of mutual connections and dynamically updated contact info. (Not to mention the fact that you don't have to pay to have it printed up.)

If you're new to Facebook, this chapter will walk you through the process of creating an account, customizing your profile, and setting your status update.

And if you're already on Facebook, you can use this chapter as a reference on how to edit and update your profile, change your basic account info (including your password), and customize the options for receiving e-mail notifications from Facebook.

Registering with Facebook

Before you join Facebook, there are a few things you might want to have at the ready—just so you don't wind up with an annoying case of *Facebookus interruptus*.

First of all, you'll need a working e-mail address. Facebook will send a confirmation message to you that you'll need to respond to as part of the setup process. So make sure to use an address that you can actually check while you're signing up.

You'll also need your date of birth, because you have to be older than 13 to join Facebook. And you might want to have a digital photo ready to use as your profile picture (although you can hold off on that till later if you want).

Once you've got those prerequisites in order, the first step to joining Facebook is to point your browser to www.facebook.com, where you'll see the Facebook login page.

No Need to Get Personal

Remember that on Facebook, profiles are used to represent individuals, and Pages are used to represent bands, businesses, and other collective entities. Pages are also the way to go for public figures, politicians, and celebrities who need to communicate with large groups of fans. So if you're looking to set up a presence for your company or group, or you're representing a public figure, you should set up a Page instead of a profile. (Of course you can still set up a personal profile for yourself.)

Also, if you're joining Facebook for work reasons—in order to set up a presence for your company, brand, or employer, for example—and you don't need or want to set up a personal profile, you can create a business account instead.

See the *Pages and Ads* chapter for full details on creating Pages and business accounts.

facebook

Remember Me   Forgot your password?

Email   Login

Facebook helps you connect and share with the people in your life.

Sign Up
It's free and anyone can join

Full Name:
Your Email:
New Password:
I am: Select Sex:
Birthday: Month: Day: Year:
Why do I need to provide this?

Sign Up

By clicking Sign Up, you are indicating that you have read and agree to the Terms of Use and Privacy Policy.

Facebook © 2008   English (US)

About   Advertising   Developers   Jobs   Terms   ▪   Find Friends   Privacy   Help

Sign Up
It's free and anyone can join

Full Name: [   ]

Your Email: [   ]

New Password: [   ]

I am: [Select Sex: ⬍]

Birthday: [Month: ⬍] [Day: ⬍] [Year: ⬍]

Why do I need to provide this?

[**Sign Up**]

Signing up for Facebook begins with filling out this simple form.

NOTE: Although you do need to specify your year of birth to join Facebook (primarily so that Facebook knows you're old enough to use the service), you don't have to display it on your profile. You're allowed to hide your age from others on Facebook if you want to. See the "Editing Your Personal and Contact Info" section for details.

Fill out the form on the right side of the page as follows:

1. Type in your full name. It has to be your real name, not a pseudonym or alias. (See the "The Importance of Being Earnest.")
2. Type in your e-mail address.
3. Choose and enter a secure password—one that contains both numbers and letters, and doesn't spell a word that can be found in a dictionary.
4. Choose Male or Female from the Select Sex menu. (You can choose not to display your gender on your profile, but at the present time Facebook does require you to specify Male or Female when you create a new account. See the "Gender Bending" sidebar for more about this.)
5. Enter your birthdate.
6. Take a deep breath and click the Sign Up button.
7. Facebook may ask you to complete a security check, which consists of typing the words shown on the screen, to prove that you're a human being and not an automatic program. If you can't read the words, Facebook gives you the option to change the words or try listening to an audio file.
8. Check your e-mail (the account you specified in step 2) for a confirmation message from Facebook. Inside the message you'll find a link to click to complete your sign-up process.

The Importance of Being Earnest (or Whatever Your Real Name Is)

As previously mentioned in the *Anatomy of Facebook* chapter, Facebook was founded on the concept of its members using their real identities, so you're required to sign up using your true legal name.

Pseudonyms and aliases are strictly a Bozo no-no. Creating what Facebook considers a "fake profile" is a violation of Facebook's Terms of Use, and grounds for deactivation.

Common nicknames like "Dave" for David or "Jenny" for Jennifer are generally fine, but signing up as Captain Creamhorn or Contessa Van Snorkel-Pudding is asking for trouble, smartypants.

Facebook takes this issue very seriously—it has a dedicated team that patrols the member rolls looking for fake profiles to deactivate. Facebook also has software that attempts to identify and block bogus names during the sign-up process.

Unfortunately, because truth is frequently more colorful than fiction, this has sometimes led to real people getting flagged for signing up with their honest-to-gosh given names. In the summer of 2008, Reuters reported on a Japanese author whose real name—Hiroko Yoda—was rejected by Facebook. Yoda is a relatively common surname in Japan, but Facebook thought she was trying to pose as Luke Skywalker's wizened Jedi master. Facebook eventually relented once Yoda proved her identity, but she's not alone: Genuine last names like Jelly, Beer, and Duck have also tripped Facebook's alarms.

If you sign up using your real name and Facebook mistakenly flags it as a fake name, your best bet is to contact Facebook directly to plead your case. Click the Help link in the footer on Facebook's Home page (it's visible even if you aren't logged in); then choose Sign Up and "My name was rejected during sign up" for a link to a contact form.

Getting Started

Once you've clicked the link in the confirmation message, you'll arrive at Facebook's Getting Started page—or actually, page one of three.

Find Friends Already on Facebook

Step 1 of 3

Welcome Jane Musser! Your account has been created.
Facebook helps you connect with friends, family, and coworkers.
Follow the steps below to find people you already know on Facebook.

Find friends using your email address book
Searching your email address book is the fastest and most effective way to find your friends on Facebook.

Your Email:

Password:

Find Friends

We won't store your password or contact anyone without your permission.

Find people you Instant Message

Skip this step ▸

The Step 1 page gives you some quick options for finding friends who are already on Facebook. Finding friends is covered at length in the next chapter, *Friends*, so for now we're going to click the "Skip this step" link at the bottom of the page and keep going.

Fill out your Profile Info

Step 2 of 3

Enter your education history and company (if any). This information will help you find your friends on Facebook.

High School: Class Year:

College/University: Class Year:

Company:

Save

Skip this step ▸

The Step 2 page lets you fill out some basic profile information to get started with: where you went to school and where you currently work.

Gender Bending

Not everyone is comfortable identifying themselves as "male" or "female." For various reasons, some people prefer to avoid labels and gendered pronouns altogether.

Facebook used to simply use neutral pronouns for anyone it didn't know the gender of: "Dave Awl tagged themself in a photo." But rigid grammarians hated it, and Facebook's translators also complained about the difficulty of translating Facebook into other languages when no gender was specified.

So, in the summer of 2008, Facebook began requiring new members to select a gender, and gently badgering existing members who hadn't already specified one to do so. But Facebook also noted, in a posting on its official blog: "We've received pushback in the past from groups that find the male/female distinction too limiting. We have a lot of respect for these communities, which is why it will still be possible to remove gender entirely from your account, including how we refer to you in Mini-Feed."

That said, at the time of this writing I wasn't able to locate any control on Facebook that would allow you to "remove gender entirely from your account." The closest thing is an option to not display your gender on your profile. (Go to the Info tab on your Profile and click the Pencil icon to edit your Basic info; then deselect the "Show my sex in my profile" checkbox.) Other than that, you can try contacting Facebook directly and asking them to allow you to go gender-neutral.

Just as in Step 1, you can choose to skip this step if you want. You can use the pop-up menu to choose a class year for your schools.

On the next page (which is still part of Step 2, if you're keeping score), Facebook will show you some names and faces of people it thinks you might know, based on whatever school or company info you provided. If you recognize anyone shown, you can click to select them, and then click the Add as Friend button to send them a friend request.

Step 3 gives you the option of typing the name of your current city or metropolitan area to join its Network. For now, skip this step—joining Networks is covered in detail in the following chapter.

Once you're done with all three steps, you'll arrive at your shiny new, largely blank, Facebook Home page. From here, you can start customizing your profile, or start searching for friends to add.

But before we invite any friends over to visit your new Facebook profile, let's spruce the place up a little by adding some information and making sure your basic account settings are in order.

Editing Your Profile

Whether you're setting up your profile for the first time or editing your existing information, Facebook's controls are basically the same.

If you've just completed the registration process, you'll find that Facebook gives you a handy "View and edit your profile" link on your new Home page so you can start filling in your profile info right away. (Clicking Profile in the blue bar will get you the same results, but let's not look a gift link in the mouth.)

Once you've added some info, it's easy to add to it or change it.

TIP: Many of the Edit controls on Facebook are hidden by default, to keep the place looking tidy. So until you mouse over them, you'd never know they were there. If you're wondering how to change or edit something, it never hurts to run your pointer over it and see if a Pencil icon magically appears.

Adding a Profile Picture

If you're adding a profile picture for the first time, you'll see a couple of quick links on the placeholder in the picture area of your profile.

Choosing Upload a Profile Picture opens a dialog that lets you browse to an existing picture on your computer.

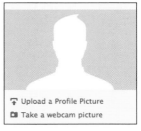

Facebook puts a couple of handy links on the picture placeholder to help you add your first profile picture.

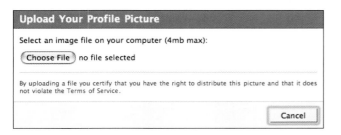

If you have a camera connected to your computer, you can choose "Take a webcam picture" and snap a quick portrait of yourself.

When you click "Take a webcam picture," the Take a Profile Picture dialog will open. It asks you to give Facebook permission to access your camera. Once you give it the green light, you're ready for your close-up.

Changing Your Profile Picture

If you want to change your profile picture, go to your Profile page and move your pointer over your current picture. You'll see the Change Picture link appear. Click that, and you'll get a menu of options for choosing from your existing pictures or uploading a new one.

*Left: The Change Picture control appears when you mouse over your profile picture.
Right: The pop-up menu gives you a bunch of useful options for changing your picture.*

Editing Your Personal and Contact Info

To edit (or add to) any of the information shown on your Info tab, you have two options. To make all of the information editable at once, click the Edit Information link at the top of the tab.

This will switch you to the editable view, which gives you various fields and menus for changing your info.

Thumbnail and I

What's the Edit Thumbnail option in the Change Picture menu all about? Facebook uses your profile picture as an avatar to represent you in various places around the site, like the News Feed and within apps. This avatar version of you is usually square, and might crop your shot a little bit to fit the correct proportions. The Edit Thumbnail option lets you choose exactly how your shot will be cropped.

Plain and Fancy

Facebook doesn't allow you to do much customization of your profile's visual design. Its philosophy is that keeping a neat, clean design that's consistent across the site helps people find what they're looking for more easily, and generally makes for a more pleasant browsing experience.

This makes neat freaks happy but is sometimes disorienting to people who come to Facebook from MySpace and expect to have the same control over colors, fonts, and layout—as well as their visitors' musical environment, with songs that start playing automatically.

But on Facebook, the idea is to express yourself with the content and information you post, rather than the design of your Profile page. You can jazz up the personality of your profile by adding fun applications, posting eye-catching photos and videos, and of course, engaging in colorful (not to say off-color) banter on your Wall.

Once you've switched to this editable view, you can click the gray bar for each section of your profile info to expand and edit it.

> ▶ **Personal Information**
>
> ▶ **Contact Information**
>
> ▶ **Education and Work**

On the other hand, if you're looking to edit one specific section, you can take the direct route by moving your pointer over the right side of the Info column for that section until the Pencil icon appears.

> **Basic Information**
>
> Networks: Chicago, IL
>   Bradley Alum
>   Neo-Futurists   Edit ✎
>
> Birthday: May 12

You can also edit the boxes that appear by default on your Wall and Info tabs, such as the Information box and the Friends box. Click the Pencil icon in the upper-right corner of any box for a pop-up menu with options related to that box.

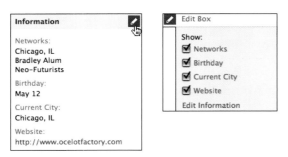

Left: The Pencil icon in the Information box. Right: The menu options for the Information box let you pick and choose what info appears there.

TIP: If you're not crazy about broadcasting your age to the world, you can hide it on your profile. Go to your Info tab, click the Pencil icon to edit your Basic Information section, and then choose "Show only month & day in my profile" from the pop-up menu under your birthday.

Book of Lists
Conventional wisdom says that putting ridiculously long lists of favorite bands or movies on your profile is the mark of a Facebook newbie. Experienced Facebookers are supposed to just toss out a few desert island picks to give you a sense of their taste and call it a day. But I've been on Facebook for a full year now, and still have somewhere around 70,000 of my favorite bands listed on my profile—so what's my excuse? In some cases, long lists may just mean that you're a compulsive, unrepentant geek.

One change you can make to the layout of your profile is that you're allowed to rearrange the locations of the boxes—some of them, anyway. The Information box and Friends box are fixed in place, but the boxes for apps such as Photos, Notes, and Posted Items can be moved. Just grab the blue title bar and drag the box until you see a dashed outline appear around a possible destination. Then release the mouse button to drop the box in its new location.

Adding a Relationship

If you've got a significant other, the two of you can declare your relationship on Facebook for all your friends to see.

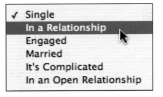

NOTE: For the process below to work, your significant other needs to be on Facebook and in your Friends list. If they aren't, you'll need to badger them to sign up and friend you. Otherwise, although you can still change your relationship status, it won't include the name of your significant other.

Go to the Info tab and click the Pencil icon to edit the Basic Information section. Using the Relationship Status pop-up menu, choose the option that best describes your relationship.

Once you choose anything other than Single from the menu, a With field will appear below the Relationship menu.

The options in the Relationship menu

Relationship Status:	In a Relationship ▲▼ with…
	Start typing a friend's name
Interested in:	

You can type the name of your sweet baboo in the box and then press Enter. Facebook will ask your baboo to confirm your relationship, and once they do, a News Feed story will be generated announcing it to the world (or at least the slice of it in your Friends list).

The "Write Something About Yourself" Box

Just under your picture on your Profile page is a little box containing the words "Write something about yourself." Click inside the box to type a short message.

This is your soapbox for whatever message you'd like to communicate, so be creative. It might be a biographical statement, a pithy quip, or a personal motto. You can also use this box to plug a current project or event, or draw attention to the link for your blog or Web site.

The "Write something about yourself" box lives just underneath your profile picture.

TIP: If you've got an all-time favorite status update you've written, and it's not time-sensitive, you might want to recycle it for duty in the "Write something about yourself" box.

Setting Your Status

Whenever you're ready to start sharing your deep thoughts, silly quips, or random cranial hiccups with your friends, you can set your first status update. You can do this easily on either your Profile page or the Home page by typing whatever you want in the Update Status field (which you'll find toward the top of both of those pages). Maybe something like, "Herman Orff is new to Facebook. Be gentle with me."

There's much more info about status updates and how to have fun with them in the *Wall, Status, and News Feeds* chapter.

Editing Your Account Info

Your basic account info is always accessible on the Account Settings page. To get there, hover your pointer over Settings in the blue bar, and then choose Account Settings. On the first tab, Settings, you can update your name if it changes (after a wedding, for example). You can also change the e-mail address where you receive notifications, change your password, add a security question, store a credit card number for buying gifts, and deactivate your account if need be.

The Meaning of *Is*

You'll notice that the word *is* appears in the Update Status field by default. That's Facebook's attempt to steer you toward answering the question you see in the box, "What are you doing right now?" The *is* used to be mandatory, but after enough pressure from users who chafed under the tyranny of the present tense, Facebook eventually yielded and made it so you can delete the *is* if you don't want it is-ing around. So go ahead and draw on the whole glorious range of verbs in the English language—past, present, and future. "Herman Orff went for a walk along the Thames," "Herman Orff thinks that cabbage in the refrigerator may have gone a bit dodgy," and "Herman Orff will get started on his third novel tomorrow" are all viable tacks to take.

TIP: Remember that whatever you type in the Update Status field will be not only displayed on your Profile page, but visible in the News Feeds of your friends. You may be startled by how quickly you get comments in response from your friends, especially if you ask a question, say something enigmatic, or otherwise tickle their fancy.

Wall in Good Time

Wondering how to edit or control what stories and posted items appear on your Wall? Don't worry, it's all covered in the *Wall, Status, and News Feeds* chapter.

Changing Notification Settings

In addition to the Notification messages that appear within the Facebook site itself (as discussed in the previous chapter), Facebook sends you notifications as e-mail messages. When someone adds you as a friend, writes on your Wall, sends you an Inbox message, posts a photo that's tagged with your name, or does any of a variety of other things Facebook thinks you might want to know about, you'll get a heads-up when you check your e-mail.

If you don't want these notifications, you can choose to turn them off —and you can pick and choose what types of Notification e-mails you receive.

To change your Notifications settings, go to Settings > Account Settings, and click the Notifications tab. You'll see a page full of radio buttons for the specific events Facebook can notify you about, letting you choose "On" (meaning you'll get an e-mail when the event takes place) or "Off" (meaning you won't) for each one.

Some of the settings for e-mail notifications on the Settings > Account Settings > Notifications page. There are also specific settings for actions related to photos, Groups, Pages, Events, Notes, videos, and more.

3

Friends

In the previous chapters you've signed up with Facebook, and learned how to set up and edit your profile. So far, so good. But if that's all there were to Facebook, there wouldn't be much point to it. It's friends, after all, who put the "social" in social networking.

So it's time to make some friends. Of course, chances are good that you signed up with Facebook because you got an invitation from a friend, and if you accepted it, then you've probably already got at least one friend displaying on your profile.

Then again, it's possible that you're starting with a clean slate—that you registered with Facebook because you keep reading news stories about it, or you stumbled across it in a Web search, or maybe you have a teenage daughter or son who keeps talking about it and you're curious what the appeal might be.

In either case, to get the most out of Facebook, you'll want to be connected to a number of friends with whom you can communicate, interact, share photos, play games, and more. How large or small that list of Facebook friends grows is entirely up to you.

Some of your friends are probably on Facebook already. Others may not be, but you can invite them to come join in the fun. And once

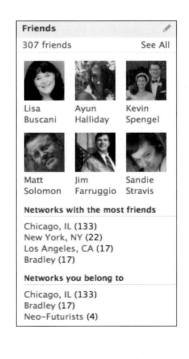

you've built up your Friends list a little, you can create special lists to keep track of them, you can introduce friends to other friends, and you can use existing friends to help you find your way to long-lost friends and make brand-new ones.

That's what this chapter is all about.

Connecting with Networks

Before you start connecting yourself to individual friends, it's a good idea to begin by connecting yourself to one or more communities that you already belong to in the 3D world: your schools, your workplace, or the city where you live. Facebook calls these communities *Networks*.

Networks and Privacy
Once you've joined a Network, you can also use it as a way to control privacy settings for a variety of Facebook features, such as who can find you by searching Facebook, or who can view photos or specific applications installed on your profile. You might create an album of photos from your college debate team, for example, and specify that it can be viewed by anyone who belongs to your school's Network as well as your friends. (See the *Privacy and Security* chapter for the full scoop on how to control specific privacy settings.)

Networks play an important role on Facebook because although Facebook has millions of members around the world, only a fraction of them can view your profile at any given time. Even though Facebook is no longer limited to college students as it was in its early days, it's held on to the principle of limiting your exposure to just the people you already know, or to people whom you might be likely to encounter in real life. That way your profile isn't hanging out there for the whole world to see—which makes using Facebook a little more private than setting up a home page on the open Web.

By default, Facebook makes your profile visible to people you've added as friends, or to anybody who belongs to a Network you've joined. In this way, Networks allow you to open up your profile just a little bit wider, to specific groups of people who are already part of your sphere. You might meet fellow students from your school in classes or at parties. You might get to know anyone who works at your company in the normal course of doing your work, or sharing the elevator each morning. And you might find yourself striking up a conversation with someone who lives in your city on the bus, at the grocery store, or in a neighborhood cafe. Joining a Network mirrors that social dynamic within Facebook itself.

How to Join a Network

You can join Networks or leave Networks at any time by visiting the Networks tab in your account settings. On the blue bar, choose Settings > Account Settings, and then click the Networks tab.

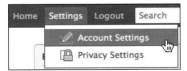

On the blue bar, choose Settings > Account Settings, and then click the Networks tab.

Once you arrive at the Networks tab, your current Networks, if any, will be listed on the page.

Network, Schmetwork

Network, Schmetwork
These days, Facebook places a lot less emphasis on Networks than it used to. Up until early 2008, the blue bar included a Networks menu, and each Network had its own home page where members could post Events, write on the Wall, and browse for local Facebook friends. Facebook says it removed the Network home pages because they weren't the most efficient way for users to connect, and the Network menu wasn't popular enough to deserve space on the blue bar. But the Networks themselves still exist, and—at least for the time being—you can still join Networks and use them to help specify settings for who can see your profile and who can't.

To join a new Network, type the name of a workplace, school, city, or region in the field on the right side of the page and click Join Network. (You may see Facebook suggest Networks for you to choose from if it begins to recognize what you're typing.)

TIP: If Facebook doesn't recognize the name you type, you'll get an error message asking you, "Please enter a valid network." Which means that a Network doesn't currently exist for the workplace, school, or community you're trying to join. If that's the case, and you feel that the community in question deserves its own Network, you can contact Facebook and request that one be created.

From there, Facebook will advise you of any requirements to join and provide instructions for completing the process.

What Networks Can You Join?

- **Regional Networks** allow you to join only one at a time. So, if you move from Chicago to San Francisco, you'll need to leave the Chicago Network before you can join the San Francisco Network.

- **College Networks** work the same way: You'll need a working address from your current school or alma mater. If you're an alumnus and you don't already have a school-issued e-mail address like *rincewind@ unseenuniversity.edu*, you'll need to set one up. (Most colleges make e-mail addresses available to alumni these days, so you can still join your alma mater's Network even if, like me, you went to college in the days of typewriters and kerosene lanterns.)

- **Workplace Networks** require you to have an actual working e-mail address from the company in order to join. So, for example, if you work for Spacely Sprockets, you'll need to be able to confirm your relationship to the company using an address such as *george@spacelysprockets.com*.

- **High School Networks** require you to be enrolled at the school before you can join them. (In order to provide maximum protection to high school–age Facebookers, it's strictly students only—even alumni and teachers aren't allowed to join high school Networks.)

Adding Friends

Stranger Danger
Before you approve any friend request, especially from someone you don't know very well, you should do a little scouting and vetting. You're allowed temporary access to the profile of anyone who sends you a friend request, so take a look at their info to make sure there isn't anything that causes you concern. Check to see if you already have any mutual friends—and if you do, you might consider sending those friends a message asking them if they can vouch for the new person or supply any useful info. If you feel any doubt or discomfort at all, then you shouldn't feel any urgency about accepting the request. Take a few days to think about it, if you need to—the request will still be there, waiting for you to accept or reject once you've made up your mind.

When someone else on Facebook wants to be your friend, you'll receive a friend request, which you'll have to approve before Facebook officially pronounces you to be pals and you show up in each other's Friends lists.

You may have received some invitations from friends before you ever joined Facebook, in which case it's possible that you may have one or more friend requests already waiting for you to respond to. But if not, you'll have plenty of friend requests to look forward to in the future.

Friend requests show up on your Home page, in the Requests area at the top of the right-hand column.

NOTE: You'll also receive an e-mail notification, unless you've tweaked your settings so as not to allow such e-mails. You can change that setting on the Settings > Account Settings > Notifications page.

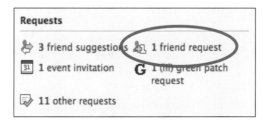

Click the request to go to the Requests page, where you can view and respond to requests.

Approving or Rejecting Friend Requests

When you receive a friend request, click the notification link on your Home page. You'll be taken to the Requests page, where any friend requests you've received but haven't approved will be displayed.

Each friend request displays the person's name, their profile picture (if they have one), and any Networks they belong to. If they've included a personal message, that will also be visible.

If you and the person who sent the request have any mutual friends on Facebook, the request will say something like, "You have 5 friends in common" (or however many there are). Notice that the phrase "5 friends" is in blue, which means you can click it to see a listing of the mutual friends. This can be a real lifesaver if your brain is having trouble making a connection to the person's name or picture, since mutual friends can clue you in to where you know the person from.

Notice that the name of the person who sent the request is also in blue, which means you can click it to go take a look at the person's profile. (Facebook grants you temporary access to the profile of anyone who sends you a friend request, even if you wouldn't normally be allowed to see it.)

It's a good idea to always check out the profile before you approve a request. If you're having trouble figuring out whether you know the person or not, it may contain clues that tip you off, like the fact that you went to the same grade school or summer camp. You might also spot red flags that suggest the person isn't someone you'd get along with, or may not be who they say they are. (See the sidebar "Stranger Danger" for more.)

Once you've made up your mind, you have two choices: Confirm, which will add the person to your Friends list and give them access to your profile, or Ignore, which will make the request go away without approving it.

If you choose to confirm the person, before you click that button you have the chance to add them to one or more Friend Lists, which help you keep your friends organized in convenient categories. (See the "Friend Lists" section, later in this chapter.) Click the "Add to Friend List" link, choose the list you want to add them to, and then click Confirm.

Once you've confirmed the person, Facebook displays a message that gives you several options. You can add Friend Details (covered in the following section), suggest friends (covered later in this chapter), or write on your new friend's Wall (see the *Wall, Status, and News Feeds* chapter.)

A friend request as it appears on the Requests page

Clicking on the number of friends you have in common reveals the names and profile pics of your mutual friends.

Click the name of the person who sent the request to check out their profile.

If you make up your mind while you're checking out the profile of the person who sent the request, you don't have to go back to the Requests page—just click the handy link underneath the person's profile picture.

Charlene Charles-Will (East Bay, CA)

You have 5 friends in common.

Add to a friend list...   ▾ (optional)

Confirm | Ignore | Send Message

Clicking "Add to a friend list" in a friend request reveals a pop-up menu that lets you add the person to any of the Friend Lists you've created.

Add Charlene to a friend list:
- Peachpit Press remove

Add to another list...

Confirm | Ignore | Send Message

You can add the same person to more than one list, so if they belong in more than one category, just click the "Add to another list" link.

You have no more friend requests.

You are now friends with Charlene Charles-Will. Add Friend Details.
Charlene is new on Facebook. To welcome her:

🐾 Suggest friends that she knows

💬 Write on her Wall

Facebook gives you a number of handy options once you've confirmed a new friend.

TIP: If you choose Ignore, keep in mind that Facebook isn't in the business of sending out rejection slips. So when you ignore someone's request, they won't get any kind of official message notifying them of that fact, and you don't have to feel like you've dumped a bucket of cold water over their head. It's true if that they're paying attention to their Friends list, eventually they may notice that you're not there and conclude that you've declined to accept them. But for all they know, you could just be way behind on your requests or still making up your mind. (And if they collar you at a party, you can always pull the old "Silly me, I must have clicked the wrong button" defense.)

There's one other action you can take if you're not ready to confirm or ignore just yet. The "Send a message" link lets you send the person a note, which you can use to request more info as to why they'd like to be your friend. Facebook alerts you to the fact that if you send the message, the person will be able to view your basic profile info for the next 30 days.

Send Message

To: Charlene Charles-Will

Subject:

Message:

Send | Cancel

If you send Charlene Charles-Will a message, you will give her permission to view your list of friends, as well as your Basic, Work and Education info for one month.

Carpe Friendem

Of course, you don't have to sit around waiting for other people to invite you. You can be proactive: Dig up people you know on Facebook using the search box and other tools, and send them friend requests yourself. I discuss how to do all that a little later in this chapter.

Adding and Editing Friend Details

Once you've added a friend, Facebook lets you add Friend Details—specific info on how, where, and when you met the person you've just friended. These details can be viewed next to their entry on your main list of friends or on any specific Friend Lists you create.

When you approve a request to add a new Friend, Facebook will give you a prompt that includes the option to add Friend Details right then and there. But even if you don't take the bait and do it in the first flush of Facebook friendship, you can always go back and add them later.

How do you know Charlene Charles-Will?

☐ Lived together   ☐ In my family
☐ Worked together   ☐ Through a friend
☐ Went to school together   ☐ We dated
☐ Traveled together   ☐ Other
☐ From an organization, team or group

[Request Confirmation] [Cancel]

The Friend Details dialog

To add or edit Friend Details, access your Friends list (always just a click away via the Friends menu in the blue bar). Find the person whose details you want to edit, and click the Toggle icon (it looks like a little box) at the right side of their listing to expand the entry.

The Toggle icon

Christopher Piatt is the last guy you want to ask about that.
on Friday

John Jughead Pierson

At the bottom of the expanded entry, you'll see your current details, or the question "How do you know *name of person*?" if there aren't any yet.

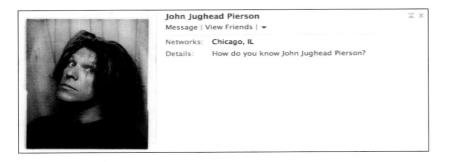

John Jughead Pierson
Message | View Friends | ▾

Networks: Chicago, IL
Details: How do you know John Jughead Pierson?

Click "edit details" if details are already present, or the question itself if they aren't. You'll get a pop-up box where you can enter various information.

Tongue in Checkbox

As you can imagine, truth frequently gives way to mirth where the Friend Details feature is concerned, and Facebook's Friends lists are littered with all sorts of fanciful (and occasionally ribald) tall tales as to how and when various individuals first crossed each other's paths. (Quite possibly the infamous "We hooked up" checkbox has been the most frequently abused, which is probably the reason it's no longer available.) But as long as both parties consent to the dirty data, anything goes. "We met at a lovely social event in the Republic of Fredonia in 1939," typed my college pal Lisa when she filled out this form, and since I always appreciate a Marx Brothers reference, I readily clicked OK.

But keep in mind that this is a two-way street, so your friend will need to approve whatever details you enter. By the same token, you'll get a notification anytime one of your friends adds or edits details about how they met you.

Selecting a checkbox in the Friend Details dialog reveals expanded controls that let you add even more details. For example, selecting "Worked together" allows you to type the name of the company where you worked and to specify the years when you were co-workers.

Use the search field on the blue menu bar to find your friends quickly.

Serious Sleuthing

If basic and advanced search aren't enough to turn up your friends, never fear. Facebook offers a slew of other advanced tools for searching up your friends on the "Find Your Friends on Facebook" page. See the "How to Pump Up Your Friends List" section, later in this chapter, for full details.

Sending a Friend Request

Now that you've taken care of the friend requests you've received, it's time to send some out yourself. Odds are good that you know plenty of Facebook members who aren't yet aware you've arrived—so all you have to do is find them. Fortunately, Facebook makes that easy with the handy search field that lives at the right side of the blue bar.

Start by thinking up names of one or more close, trusted friends. (Feel free to jot a short list on a sticky note or a napkin or something.) Type the first person's name into the search field and hit Return/Enter. You may get a list of several similarly named people, or one name if your friend has a very distinctive monicker. (If you get multiple results, see the sidebar "Needle in a Friendstack" for tips on figuring out which one is your pal.)

If it turns out that your friend isn't on Facebook yet, you'll get a message telling you there aren't any results for that name, with the option to search by other factors (including e-mail address, school, or company), or to send an invite to your friend.

You can also click the Profile Search link, which takes you to an Advanced Profiles Search form that allows you to search by all kinds of very specific factors, up to and including favorite TV shows. (This could take a lot of the sweat out of tracking down all those scintillating people you met at the Battlestar Galactica convention last year.) But the catch is that Advanced Profile Search is limited to only people who belong to one of the Networks you're in, so if you don't share an alma mater, an employer, or a ZIP code with the person you're looking for, it may not help you much.

The Advanced Profiles search form

Your 5,000 Closest Friends

How many friends can one human being have? On Facebook, the answer is easy: 5,000. As celebrities as diverse as Stephen Fry and Yoko Ono have discovered, Facebook places a firm limit of 5,000 on the number of friends you can add to your profile. Even Santa Claus has been stymied by that limit—according to an item on *Wired* magazine's blog, a man whose legal name is Santa Claus, and who runs an advocacy group for children called the Santa Claus Foundation, reached the 5,000 friend limit within a month of joining Facebook. And not all of his elves and reindeer working together could persuade Facebook to raise the ceiling. (The item noted that Facebook did cut him a break by allowing him to sign up as "Santa Claus" in the first place, once he proved that it was his legal name.)

Facebook's position is that your profile's Friends list should emphasize personal relationships with people you actually know. But if you're a public figure or politician whose fans and supporters number in the thousands, don't despair: Facebook has a solution for you. You can set up what's called a Facebook Page. Facebook Pages are free, and they look like profiles, but they give you more powerful tools for communicating with and keeping track of your enormous fan base. And you won't have to spend all your time approving endless friend requests, either: When someone chooses to become a fan or supporter of your Facebook Page, the approval is automatic. (After all, if you're a rock star, you don't get to choose who wears your band's T-shirt.) See the *Pages and Ads* chapter for full info on how to set up and manage Facebook Pages.

The Add as Friend link appears at the right side of the entry for each person who turns up in your search results—unless they're already your friend, of course.

TIP: When someone you've added accepts your friend request, you'll get a message letting you know on your Notifications page.

Once you do identify someone you know and want to bond with, all you have to do is click the Add as Friend link next to their entry in the results. The Add Friend dialog will appear.

Add Rod as a friend?

Rod will have to confirm that you are friends.

Add a personal message...

Add to a friend list...   ▼ (optional)

[Add Friend]   [Cancel]

The Add Friend dialog. You can choose a Friend List from the pop-up menu, and your friend will be added to the list once they've confirmed you.

You'll have the option to type a short message to your friend—which I highly recommend doing if there's any chance they might not recognize or remember you by name. If it's someone you know only slightly, or an old school chum you lost track of two decades ago, you'll earn good karma (and possibly a faster approval of your request) by erring on the side of providing their brain with a little context—which will give them the opportunity to respond with something graceful like, "How could I possibly forget you?" even as they're silently thanking you for not making them scrape their gray matter to come up with the reason your name rings a bell.

Add Rod as a friend?

Rod will have to confirm that you are friends.

Add a personal message: Cancel

[   ]

Add to a friend list...   ▼ (optional)

[Add Friend]   [Cancel]

Clicking on the words "Add a personal message" in the Add Friend dialog opens up a field where you can type a personal note—so your friend request seems a little less out of the blue.

Once you've submitted your request, you can search for other friends and lather/rinse/repeat to your heart's content. Then sit back and wait for the love to roll in.

Inviting Friends Who Aren't on Facebook

Inevitably, at least a few of your favorite people won't be on Facebook yet. If that's the case, maybe it's your destiny to recruit them. You can easily invite anyone you want to join Facebook, as long as you know their e-mail address and they're over 13 years of age.

Finding a Needle in a Friendstack

So you typed "Joe Smith" or "Amy Johnson" into the Facebook search field and surprise, surprise, you got a huge list of people to choose from. How do you know which if any of the results is your own personal Joe or Amy?

If they've posted an accurate picture, it shouldn't be too hard to pick them out of the lineup. But if they're camera shy, they may have chosen to hide behind a picture of a family pet or a favorite cartoon character—or they may have no picture at all—in which case you'll need to do a little sleuthing.

Facebook tries to help you by sorting the most likely results to the top of the list—so anyone who belongs to one of your Networks will be listed first. That means that if your friend went to your high school or college, works at your company, or lives in your town, odds are good they're higher on the page rather than lower.

But suppose you met this particular friend while backpacking in New Zealand last year and don't have any Network factors in common. In that case, it's time to break out the big magnifying glass. Take a look under each person's name—if they belong to any Networks, those will be listed. You might be able to identify your friend by their geographic location, or their school or company.

If that doesn't work, the best clue left to you at this point is mutual friends. Unless they've hidden it in their privacy settings (see the *Privacy and Security* chapter for details on that), you should see a View Friends link on the right side of each person's entry. Clicking it will show you their Friends list. If you can spot your friend's significant other, sibling, roommate, sidekick, or anyone else you both know, you've got a bull's-eye.

If all else fails, you've still got the option of sending a polite inquiry to whomever seems most likely to be the person you're looking for. Click the Send a Message link and compose a bashful missive along the lines of, "Forgive me if I've got the wrong person, but are you the Amy Johnson I used to steal Tater Tots from during 'C' lunch period in 1985? If so, I think I owe you a bag or two of Idaho's finest . . . "

Navigate to your Facebook Home page and scroll down to the link that says Invite Your Friends toward the bottom of the right-hand column. Click that link and you'll be taken to a page with an easy form to fill out.

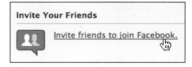

The Invite Your Friends link on the Home page

Invite Your Friends

From:	Dave Awl
To: (use commas to separate emails)	
Message: (optional)	

Import Email Addresses ▸
from your Yahoo, Hotmail, AOL, Gmail, MSN, Live.com or Comca address book.

Hotmail Gmail
YAHOO! Mail AOL

View All Invites ▸
See your entire history of invitations, including who has joined because of you.

Invites will be sent in English. [change]

[Invite] [Cancel]

If a friend you're inviting would be more comfortable viewing Facebook in a different language, use the pop-up menu to choose the best language for the invitation.

In the top field, type the e-mail addresses of the people you want to invite, separated by commas. In the bottom field, type an optional message to the recipients. If desired, you can change the language in which the invite will be sent by clicking the "[change]" link next to "Invites will be sent in English." Click Invite to finish, or Cancel if you're having second thoughts, and you're done.

There are two other options you'll notice on the Invite Your Friends page. Import E-mail Addresses lets you invite a batch of friends from various online address books you might use. See the "How to Pump Up Your Friends List" section later in this chapter for more info.

The View All Invites link in the lower-right corner of the form takes you to the Invite History page, which lets you see all the people you've invited to Facebook in the past, including who has accepted your invitation and who hasn't—yet. (Don't be surprised if people who don't accept your invitation right away eventually pop up on Facebook many months later.)

![Invite History page showing a list of sent invitations with Send Reminder links and dates]

The Invite History page shows you all the Facebook invitations you've sent at a glance, and lets you send reminders if you want to follow up on the ones that haven't been accepted.

Personalize It

When you're inviting someone to join Facebook, you'll almost always get better results if you take advantage of the optional message field. Type a short personal greeting that demonstrates to the person (or persons) you're inviting that it's really you, and not a spammer, that's sending the invitation. Addressing them by name and working in a reference to how you know them, a mutual friend, or an in-joke are good ways to boost the credibility of the invite.

The Invite History page comes with various management tools. You can select the checkboxes next to the names of anyone you want to remove from the list, and then click Delete Selected at the top of the list. You can send reminders to those who haven't responded by clicking the Send Reminder link next to their name, or selecting their checkbox and clicking Send Reminder at the top of the list.

The Select menu lets you automatically select the checkboxes for everyone, no one, or just those who haven't yet joined Facebook. The Sort By menu lets you choose the order in which your invitees are displayed: by name, by date of invitation, or by whether or not they've accepted your invite.

Suggesting Friends

If you have two Facebook friends who know each other in the real world but haven't found their way into each other's Friends lists yet, Facebook gives you a handy way to point them out to each other.

You can also use this feature to play Facebook Cupid, and introduce two people who don't know each other yet, but whom you're pretty sure will be likely to hit it off. If you go that route, however, you should exercise a little discretion—and by all means send an introductory message, as discussed in the "Suggestion Box" etiquette note on the following page.

To suggest friends, go to the profile of the person you'd like to suggest as a friend for someone else. If the person has recently joined Facebook, you'll see a "Suggest Friends for *name*" link underneath their profile photo. If they're a Facebook veteran, it won't be quite so prominent, but you can still find it toward the bottom of their profile (make sure you're on the Wall or Info tab).

Click the link and you'll be presented with a form that allows you to choose the people you want to send messages to.

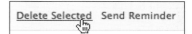

The links at the top of the Invite History page

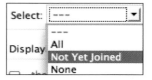

The options in the Select menu on the Invite History page

The options in the Sort By menu on the Invite History page

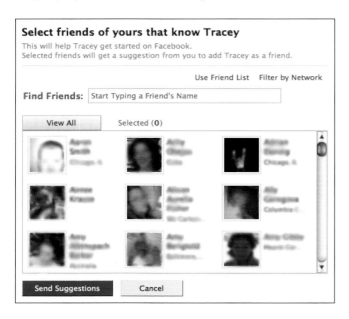

The Suggest Friends link

View All	Selected (4)

☒ You are viewing 131 friends in Chicago, IL

	Timothy		Tina

Click the X to remove the Network filter.

Suggestion Box

If you suggest a friend for someone, unless you're 100 percent sure that they already know the person you're suggesting, as a matter of courtesy you should send the person who will be receiving the suggestion a friendly little note telling them exactly why you think they might want to befriend the person in question. Otherwise they'll be stuck looking at a person whose name and picture they don't recognize, scratching their head and wondering whether they've met them before.

You might expect Facebook to include an option to do this on the Friend Suggestion form itself, but as of this writing it isn't there, so you'll need to send a separate Inbox message. See the *Communicating on Facebook* chapter for the skinny on sending messages to your Facebook friends.

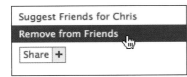

The dreaded Remove from Friends link—Facebook's equivalent of the pink slip

You can click "Use Friend List" to choose recipients from a Friend List you've created (see the section on Friend Lists later in this chapter) or click "Filter by Network" to see just potential recipients who belong to a certain Network. (You can reverse the filtering process by clicking the little X next to the words "You are viewing *number* friends in *name of Network*." Clicking the X takes you back to the All Friends view.)

Once you've chosen the people you want to send the suggestion to, click "Send Suggestions," and you're done.

So, for example, let's say that your friend Tracey has just popped up on Facebook, and you have a number of mutual friends who'd be glad to know she's arrived. Go to Tracey's profile, click the Suggest Friends link, and send a message to all of Tracey's other fans among your Facebook friends. Facebook will reward you with a notification when any friendships you recommend are actually consummated.

If, on the other hand, you'd like to introduce your friends Lisa and Amy to each other, you'll need to pick which one gets the message. So, let's say that you'd like to send a message to Lisa recommending that she add Amy as a friend. In that case, you'll go to Amy's profile, click the Suggest Friends link, and select Lisa to receive the message.

> **NOTE:** Some users find the direction in which Friend Suggestions travel to be a little bit counterintuitive—when they click the link that says "Suggest Friends for Amy" on Amy's profile, they expect to be sending a message *to* Amy suggesting possible people for her to befriend. Just keep in mind that it works the other way around—the link sends a suggestion *about* the person in question, not *to* them.

Removing a Friend

If you decide that you need to "de-friend" someone, removing them from your list of friends altogether, there are a number of easy ways to break up. (I'm not sure if there are 50 ways or not—you'd have to ask Paul Simon.) Here are two of the simplest: You can go directly to the person's profile and click the "Remove from Friends" link toward the bottom of the page, or you can find their entry in your Friends list and click the "X" button over on the right-hand side.

Either way, you'll get a dialog asking you to confirm that you really want to give this person the heave-ho. (This step can't be undone—at least not without crawling to your brand new ex-friend and begging them to refriend you—so make sure you really want to do it before you click Confirm.)

The Remove Friends dialog asks you if you're sure you really want to do that.

If you do defriend someone, they won't receive any kind of official notification message, so the only way they'll find out about it—assuming you don't tell them—is if they go looking for you in their Friends list and discover you've gone missing.

Viewing Your Friends

By default, Facebook displays a little sampler of six randomly chosen friends in the Friends box that appears on the Wall and Info tabs of your profile. A different selection displays every time the page is loaded, unless you change that (see below).

You can set some additional options for the Friends box by clicking the Edit (pencil) icon in the upper-right corner:

- Use the Show menu to choose the number of friends who are displayed (the choices are 6, 9, or 12).
- The "Always show these friends" option lets you type the names of a few of your bestest pals that you want to always show in the box.
- The "Include friends from" checkboxes let you choose to include or exclude specific Networks when Facebook chooses random friends to display. So if you want to hide all co-workers from your office or all classmates from a certain school, you can deselect those boxes. (But note that this will only work if the people in question have joined the relevant Networks. So if you have a classmate from Riverdale High who never joined the Riverdale Network, they might still show up even if you deselect the Riverdale box.)
- The Show Networks Section checkbox lets you show or hide a listing of the various Networks your friends fall into.

To see all of your friends at once, click the See All link in the upper-right corner of the Friends box, or click the word "Friends" in the blue menu bar.

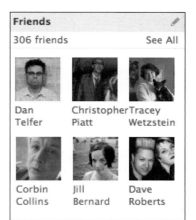

The Friends box as it appears by default

Click the Pencil icon to set options for the Friends box.

Setting options in the dialog for the Friends box

The Friends box with nine random friends and the Networks section displaying.

Some of the options in the Everyone view's pop-up menu

In either case, you'll be taken to your main Friends page, with the default All Friends list displayed.

The view options along the top of the All Friends list

You can sort the All Friends list using the links across the top:

- **Status Updates** shows friends who recently updated their status.
- **Recently Updated** shows you friends who've made changes to their profiles.
- **Phonebook** gives you a handy listing of phone numbers for your friends. (Numbers will only show up for those who've chosen to include them in their profile and make them visible to you. See the *Privacy and Security* chapter for info on how to control who can see your phone number.)
- **Everyone** shows you your entire list of friends, in alphabetical order by last name. If you have many friends, they may be broken into several pages. You can use the number menu at the top right of the list to navigate between pages within the list.

At the top of the Everyone view of the All Friends list, there's a menu that lets you choose from even more options for viewing your friends—sorting them by the Networks they belong to, or by Friend Details you've added.

Choosing the generic Network options (College Friends, Work Friends, and so on) will cause a "from" submenu to appear, from which you can further specify. For example, once you choose Regional Friends, you can then choose a specific local Network from the menu, so that you can see just your friends in Milwaukee or Austin or New York, for example.

The choices in the bottom half of the menu depend on the Friend Details you and your friends have supplied. (See "Adding and Editing Friend Details," earlier in this chapter.) Choosing Travel Buddies, for instance, will display anyone for whom you selected the "Traveled together" checkbox when editing the Friend Details dialog (or anyone who selected that checkbox for you, if they did the editing most recently).

Note that these lists are automatically generated and rely on the quality of information provided. If you or a friend fibbed about how you met or didn't supply any info, you won't get 100 percent accurate results. See the section on Friend Lists, later in this chapter, for how to create lists that you can organize and manage yourself.

The Politics of Friending

How many Facebook friends should you have? And should you friend people you don't know very well, or limit your Friends list to proven pals?

As with so many questions in life, there's no absolute right or wrong answer to that question—it all depends on what you personally are comfortable with.

Some people take a "more the merrier" approach, approving every friend request automatically, and sending invitations to anyone and everyone who seems remotely interesting.

At the other end of the scale are the people who prefer to keep a small, carefully pruned Friends list consisting of only their nearest and dearest—the people they feel they could be happy living on a small wooden raft with. No strangers or casual acquaintances need apply.

And then there are the rest of us, who fall somewhere along the spectrum between those two extremes.

When I first joined Facebook, I had the idea that my Friends list would be limited to only people I knew fairly well. The first time a complete stranger sent me a friend request, I wasn't sure what to do. Fortunately, I was able to deduce by looking at our mutual friends that the person in question was a fan of my old theater company, and after approving his request I was glad I got to know him.

As I continued to get similar requests, I concluded that it wasn't in my interest as a writer and performer to reject people who liked my work. So I decided to think of my profile as more public than private, and simply avoid posting anything I wouldn't choose to share with the whole world on my public Web site. For me personally, Facebook has proved to be a great place to make new friends, in addition to reconnecting with old ones.

Your mileage may vary, of course. Ultimately, only you can decide exactly where you fall on the scale between "the more the merrier" and "less is more." But thinking about the following questions can help you make up your mind about how social you want to be.

1. **How introverted or extroverted are you?**

If you've ever taken the Myers-Briggs Type Indicator test, then you may already have a good sense of whether you generally chart as an extrovert or an introvert. But even if you're muttering, "The Myers what now?" at the moment (Google is your friend), you should have some sense of whether you're the outgoing sort who likes to surround yourself with tons of friends, or the quiet type who feels more comfortable with a smaller social set.

Of course, just because you're shy in the real world doesn't mean you're that way online. Some people find that the Internet liberates them to be more outgoing, and feel more confident expressing themselves in writing than speaking. If you're the sort who blossoms socially when you go online, then your Facebook Friends list may quickly outgrow your offline address book.

2. **How open to making new friends are you at this stage of your life?**

Even if you're generally a people person, you might find yourself at an age where you're already surrounded with dear old friends you never have enough time for, so don't feel the urge to make a lot of new ones.

On the other hand, if you've just moved to a new community or are feeling like your social scene could use some new energy, then making new friends might be moving up your list of priorities with a bullet.

3. **How conservative do your employers or your profession require you to be?**

The news has been rife with stories of people who've gotten in trouble for posting something they probably shouldn't have to their Facebook profile, MySpace page, or personal blog. Some companies do keep tabs on their employees' Internet presence—especially if they access their profiles on company time or use them in the course of their work.

If your co-workers or your boss are on Facebook, that provides some added incentive to make sure your profile hews to a professional image. And even if you're still in school, or not currently working for a large company, it pays to think ahead a little. Everyone should know by now that employers sometimes check out the Facebook and MySpace profiles of job candidates, looking for red flags before they make final hiring decisions.

Obviously there are some professions that require you to keep more of a clean-cut, button-down image than others. If you're a musician, a massage therapist, or an interior decorator, you may have a little more freedom of self-expression than if you're the local pastor or a lawyer hoping to become district attorney one day.

Of course, even if the above considerations apply to you, keeping your Friends list on the small side isn't the only way to avoid getting into trouble. Facebook gives you a variety of specific tools and settings to control who can view certain photos, applications, or information on your profile. (See the *Privacy and Security* chapter for the full details on those controls.) And there's no substitute for exercising some basic caution about what you post in the first place.

4. **Does your livelihood depend on exposure and staying on other people's radar?**

Some careers thrive by staying in view of other people. If you're a musician, actor, comedian, or writer, for example, then you want to build a following of fans, and remind the various colleagues, agents, producers, directors, and editors who can hook you up with work that you exist. Facebook can be an excellent way to keep yourself in other people's line of sight.

By the same token, if you're an independent professional, freelancer, or entrepreneur of any kind, Facebook can help you keep in touch with your clients, co-workers, and other members of your professional network, so that you're top of mind when they're looking to hire someone.

On the other hand, if you're a public figure with a very large following of fans, or running a business that needs professional promotion, then you might want to consider setting up a Facebook Page for your fans and customers, and reserving your profile for personal friends only. See the *Pages and Ads* chapter for complete info on how to set them up, and how to take advantage of their sophisticated tools for communicating with fans, supporters, and customers.

Either way, it behooves you to do a little thinking at the outset about how your Facebook presence can work for you, and how public versus private you want it to be.

5. **Do you have anything you want to promote on Facebook, and is that a significant part of your reason for being on Facebook?**

This is closely related to the previous question—but if you've got a book or a film to sell, a blog or podcast to promote, a dog-walking business you're launching, a proposed local ordinance you're campaigning to defeat, or anything else you'd like to maximize word of mouth about, a larger Friends list will increase the audience for your status updates, Facebook Notes, viral videos, and other posted items.

6. **Are there people from your past (or present) you don't want to find you?**

Sometimes people have very legitimate reasons for not wanting to be found. Maybe you've got a problematic ex (or six). Maybe you're feeling antisocial these days and not in the mood to relive your high school years just now. Maybe you're in the Witness Protection Program. Maybe you're Peter Parker and you don't want Harry Osborn to track you down until he's cooled off about the dad thing a little.

Depending on the seriousness of your reasons, you may want to give a little extra thought to whether you should be on Facebook at all, and you'll want to make sure you pay a visit to the *Privacy and Security* chapter so that you can take full advantage of Facebook's privacy settings.

But it's also important to understand that as your Friends list grows, so does the set of people who are friends with your Facebook friends, increasing the likelihood that old acquaintances will spot you on a mutual friend's profile. So keeping your list small may (I stress the word *may*) help to limit your exposure somewhat.

7. **How much do you enjoy interacting with people online?**

Some people were born to chat, e-mail, and text—others prefer face-to-face interaction or using the phone. The larger your Friends list, the more likely you are to get pokes, messages, Wall posts, application requests, and other virtual forms of communication.

I personally enjoy the semiotics of Facebook—if I didn't, I wouldn't be writing this book. I love waking up to Wall posts from college friends, SuperPokes from former co-workers, and Green Patch daffodils from friends I met while traveling the UK a few summers back.

But I've had one or two friends decide to leave Facebook simply because they didn't like responding to all the messages piling up in their Inbox, or feeling obligated to return the various pokes and plants and vampire bites they received from their friends. (If you found that last sentence puzzling, don't worry—it's all explained in upcoming chapters.)

So if you're someone who hates typing when you could be talking, keeping your Friends list small might be a way of reining in the total volume of messages you receive.

On the other hand, this is another case where friend control isn't your only option for keeping things within manageable bounds. Take a deep breath and remember:

- You're not obligated to respond to requests from anyone just because they're in your list of friends. (If your friendship doesn't survive an unreturned SuperPoke, it was probably on thin ice already.)
- There's no law saying you have to reply to a message using the same medium. If you'd rather respond to a friend's Wall post by picking up the phone and giving them a jingle, that's your prerogative, and they'll probably appreciate it just as much.
- You can uninstall any application that brings you more annoyance than pleasure.
- And you can even choose to block all requests from a specific person if you feel they're bombarding you with things you're not interested in or don't have time for.

8. How are your time-management skills?

There's a popular button in the Pieces of Flair application that reads, "Facebook—you didn't want to go outside anyway."

Hey, this is the 21st century. Even Zen monks feel rushed, overbooked, and short of time. Facebook can absolutely be part of a healthy balanced diet (like the cereal in those Saturday-morning TV commercials), and with a little self-control and moderation you can tend your Green Patch on Facebook and still make it outside to smell the nonvirtual petunias well before the sun sinks in the west.

But there's no denying that Facebook can be seriously addictive, and if you know you have a hard time saying no to playing games when you should be working, and you have the kind of obsessive personality that lets the dirty dishes and the bills pile up while you engage in Wall banter with your A-list amigos, then limiting the number of people who are empowered to distract you online might be a sensible approach.

This is the small People You May Know box that lives on the Home page. Click the "see all" link to go check out the much larger sampling on the "Find Your Friends on Facebook" page.

People You Don't Know
if you're certain you don't know a specific person, you can click the little X next to their entry to make them go away. (Don't worry—they'll never know you did it, and it won't sour your chances of becoming friends in the future if you meet them at a party or something. However, it *will* prevent you from being recommended to the person you X'ed out by their own People You May Know listing.)

How to Pump Up Your Friends List

If you're in a social mood, and you'd like to connect with as many of your real-world friends as possible on Facebook, you're in luck—Facebook gives you lots of great ways to find them and connect with them.

People You May Know

One of Facebook's best tools for finding your friends lives right on the Home page: the People You May Know tool.

Here's how it works: When you have a certain number of friends in common with another Facebook member, the system figures it's likely the two of you know each other. So Facebook serves up a regular sampler of folks who meet certain criteria (which may include such things as school and work info, in addition to mutual friends).

The People You May Know box on the Home page shows you only a few possibilities—if you want to see a much larger sampling, click the "see all" link. That will take you to the "Find Your Friends on Facebook" page, and now you're cooking with gas. In the middle of the page you'll see a super-sized helping of possible friends. If you recognize someone you know, click the "Add as Friend" link to send a friend request.

The full-size People You May Know section on the "Find Your Friends on Facebook" page gives you a much larger selection of possible friends to choose from.

If you're not sure whether you know the person or not, you can click their name or picture to check out their profile (or if you're not allowed to view the profile itself, Facebook will give you a dialog with basic info such as your mutual friends).

The People You May Know tool will show you a slightly different selection of people every time you refresh (as long as there are enough good candidates out there). So keep a close eye on it, and feel free to reload the page a few times if you want to see more people. If you're looking to build your Friends list, you might want to get into a habit of visiting the "Find Your Friends on Facebook" page on a regular basis to see who Facebook is suggesting to you.

The Friend Finder

The Friend Finder—Facebook's contact importer—also lives on the "Find Your Friends on Facebook" page. You can access it easily from the Home page by clicking the link under "Find Your Friends" at the bottom of the right-hand column.

If you use a Web-based e-mail account, this handy tool can search your address book to find friends who are already on Facebook, identifying them by their e-mail address. It works with any Webmail account from one of the following providers: Yahoo, Hotmail, AOL, Gmail, MSN, Live.com, or Comcast.

The catch is that you'll need to type in your e-mail address and the password for your Webmail account—giving Facebook temporary access to your account. Facebook promises not to store or share this info, but if you're not comfortable entering it, you'll want to take a pass on using this tool.

NOTE: The People You May Know Tool can be helpful, but it's not a sure-fire thing. One friend of mine refers to it as "People You've Been Trying to Avoid," because of its uncanny ability to serve up the people in your social circle you're not so fond of.

Find Your Friends   close

Use our contact importer to find friends you didn't know were on Facebook.

You can access the Friend Finder easily using this handy link on the Home page.

Import Email Addresses ▸

from your Yahoo, Hotmail, AOL, Gmail, MSN, Live.com or Comcast address book.

Hotmail   Gmail

YAHOO! Mail   AOL

If you use Webmail from any of the listed providers, you can access your address book using the Friend Finder.

Find people you know on Facebook

Your friends on Facebook are the same friends, acquaintances and family members that you communicate with in the real world. You can use any of the tools on this page to find more friends.

Find People You Email   Upload Contact File

Searching your email address book is the fastest and most effective way to find your friends on Facebook.

Your Email: [   ]

Password: [   ]

[Find Friends]

We won't store your password or contact anyone without your permission.

The Friend Finder lives on the "Find Your Friends on Facebook" page and makes it easy to find friends you e-mail regularly if they're on Facebook.

You can also get around the password-sharing issue by clicking the Upload Contact File link, which lets you provide Facebook with a listing of your address book contacts generated by a program such as Outlook, Thunderbird, Mac OS X Address Book, and more. (Click the "How to create a contact file" link for instructions specific to whatever program you use.)

> **Find People You Email**
> Searching your email address book is the fastest and most effective way to find your friends on Facebook.
>
> Upload a contact file and we will tell you which of your contacts are on Facebook. How to create a contact file....
>
> Outlook
> Outlook Express
> Windows Address Book
> Mozilla Thunderbird
> Palm Desktop
> Palm Desktop (vCard)
> Entourage
> Mac OS X Address Book
> LinkedIn
> Other
>
> Still having problems? Contact us.
>
> Contact File: [   ] Browse...

Facebook also gives you the option of uploading a contact file generated by your e-mail or address book program. Click "How to create a contact file" and then the name of the program you use for specific instructions.

Similarly, if you use instant message programs, you can let Facebook comb through your AIM Buddy List or Windows Live Contacts list to find people you know who've listed their IM handles on Facebook. Scroll down to the "Find People You IM" section at the bottom of the page, and click the appropriate link.

Advanced Search

You may have already searched for friends using the basic search field that lives in the blue menu bar. But there are some advanced search tools on the "Find Your Friends on Facebook" page, under the "Search for People" heading. Here you can search for classmates from your high school or college, or co-workers from your workplace Networks.

Class Consciousness
The high school and college advanced searches focus on your year of graduation by default. But if you had lots of friends older or younger than you, fear not. You can use the pop-up menu at the top of the results page to change the year and search for the seniors you worshipped or the freshmen you terrorized.

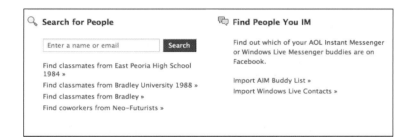

from people in Bradley 1988 ▼
2007
2006
2005
2004
2003
2002

Search for People

[Enter a name or email] Search

Find classmates from East Peoria High School 1984 »
Find classmates from Bradley University 1988 »
Find classmates from Bradley »
Find coworkers from Neo–Futurists »

Find People You IM

Find out which of your AOL Instant Messenger or Windows Live Messenger buddies are on Facebook.

Import AIM Buddy List »
Import Windows Live Contacts »

Invitations

As discussed earlier in this chapter, you can use the "Invite Your Friends" link on the Home page to send invitations to join Facebook to anyone who isn't already registered and for whom you have a current e-mail address. You might want even want to jot down a short list of your favorite pals, search for them one at a time, and if they aren't on Facebook, send them invitations.

TIP: Clicking the More Search Options link on the Results page will take you to a page where you can search for people by any school or any company—not just the ones you attended or worked for yourself.

Invitation Swarming: The Magic of Piling On

If you have a good friend you really, really want to join Facebook, and you have several mutual friends already on Facebook, there's a sneaky trick that almost always works: the coordinated attack. After all, getting one invitation from an old friend is compelling, but getting three or four on the same day feels like the stars are aligning.

I know from firsthand experience, because that's how I wound up joining Facebook myself, after getting several invitations from old friends on the same day.

So suppose at a previous job you were part of a tight-knit group of co-workers with your pals Buddy, Sally, and Rob. Buddy and Sally are already on Facebook, but for some reason Rob hasn't shown up yet. You can drop Buddy and Sally a message letting them know you're about to send Rob an invite, and suggest that they might want to send him one at around the same time. There's no guarantee that Rob will take the bait, but the odds have definitely improved.

Friends of Friends

Although Facebook's automatically generated People You May Know tool is pretty sharp, it doesn't catch everyone. So the manual approach works pretty well, too. If you're looking for old pals, one of the best places to find them is lurking in the Friends lists of mutual friends. Spend a little time clicking on your friends' Friends lists and scanning them for familiar faces. It's a small world, and you may be surprised to discover some of the friends you have in common.

Creating and Using Friend Lists

Whether you realize it consciously or not, you probably already sort your friends and acquaintances into categories. You may have one set of old friends from high school, a group of co-workers you enjoy hanging out with, and another group of friends from your church, your bowling league, or your favorite dance club.

These groupings come in handy when you're organizing social events. If you're planning a dinner party, for example, and you invite six of your old high school pals along with your friend Phil from the office, Phil might feel a little overwhelmed, especially when you're off in the kitchen carving radishes into little rosebuds and putting spray-cheese on Triscuits. So if you're a good host, you think to yourself, hmm, maybe I should invite a few more people from the office so Phil has someone to talk to while the ice is getting broken.

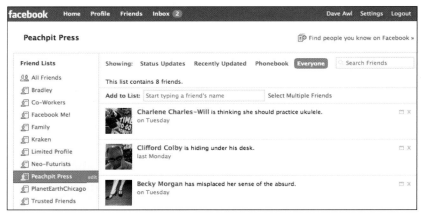

Friend Lists let you organize your friends into convenient categories.

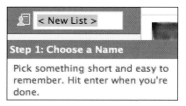

Click the Make a New List button on your Friends page to create a new Friend List.

NOTE: You won't see the Make a New List button unless you have a minimum of 11 friends. If you have ten Facebook friends or less, Facebook figures it's easy enough to keep them organized in your head.

Type a name for your new Friend List in the field that opens up.

TIP: You can delete a Friend List at any time by scrolling down to the "Delete this list" link at the bottom of the list.

Just as you do in the 3D world, Facebook's Friend Lists can help you keep track of the various categories your friends fall into—which ones already know each other, which ones would need to be introduced, and which ones are most likely to attend, say, a night at the theater, a golf outing, or a Sunday morning brunch.

In upcoming chapters, I'll show you how to use Friend Lists in all sorts of useful ways—to home in on the people you want to invite to a Facebook Event you're creating, to control which friends can see your mobile phone number or that Naughty Gifts app you just installed, and to keep tabs on the friends whose profiles you want to check on a daily or weekly basis.

For now, here's how to create a new Friend List. First, click the word "Friends" in the blue bar. You'll be taken to your main Friends page, with the All Friends list showing by default. The column along the left is where your created Friend Lists will be displayed, if and when you have any. Click the "Make a New List" button to add one.

The first step is to name your new list, so a field opens where you can type the name. Keep it short or Facebook will truncate it to fit the column, and make sure the name is something clear that won't leave you scratching your head later.

Step two is to add some friends to your newly named list. Start typing the name of the first person you'd like to add—Facebook will suggest people you know as soon as it starts to recognize what you're typing (or thinks it does, anyway). Use the arrow keys to select from the suggestions, or hit Return/Enter if there's only one candidate.

Friend Lists

👥 All Friends	Showing: **Status Updates** Recently Updated Phonebook Ever
📁 Colleagues	🧑 Dave is pushing back against the brain-burn. 20 hours ago
📁 Bradley	This list contains 38 friends.
📁 Facebook Me! edit	**Rachel Claff** wishes Michael Phelps' nutritionists would tell HER to consume 8,000–10,000 calories a day. 19 minutes ago
📁 Family	
📁 Hartmann Center	**Lori Dana** is grinding out the graphics today... 2 hours ago
📁 Kraken	
📁 Limited Profile	

Your Friend Lists appear in the left-hand column on your Friends page. Click the name of a list to display it. To change the name of a Friend List, click the "edit" link that appears next to its name when the list is selected.

You can create up to 100 different Friend Lists, and each list can contain as many as 1500 friends.

If a list has fewer than 20 people, you can use it to conveniently send a message to all the members at once. Just click the "Message this list" link at the bottom of the list itself. If the list has more than 20 members, you'll get an error message telling you it's too big. You might want to consider breaking it up into several smaller lists for messaging purposes—and since redundancy is okay on Friend Lists, there's no need to delete the original big list before you create the smaller ones.

By the way, your friends have no way of knowing what lists you do or don't add them to, so if you decide to create a list called "PWDLM" (People Who Dance Like Monkeys) or something, the people you add to it will be none the wiser. (Of course, your karma might take a hit.)

Adding a friend to a Friend List. Facebook will try to guess what you're typing and suggest names for you to choose from.

TIP: You can put the same friend on more than one list, so if Phil is in your scuba club as well as working at your office, you can add him to your "Diving Buddies" list right after you add him to "Co-workers."

NOTE: You can add only people you're already friends with to a Friend List. If you type the name of someone you haven't already bonded with on Facebook, you'll get a "no matches found" message.

Cleaning Up a List

If you accidentally add someone to a list who doesn't belong there, you can click the small X at the right of their entry to remove them, but be careful to click "Remove from List" in the dialog—if you accidentally click "Remove from Friends," you'll wind up de-friending them altogether. (Of course, if that's what you *want* to do, knock yourself out.)

To Friend or Not to Friend—When You're on the Fence

Facebook brings with it some tricky and unexpected dilemmas. You'll get plenty of no-brainer friend requests from your best chums, and some wonderfully out-of-the-blue invitations from long-lost friends you've been missing for years.

But you'll also get some that make you scratch your head a little. Should you be Facebook friends with your boss? Your in-laws? Your old college roommate's mom? The kid from your grade school who made you eat a live centipede and apparently now wants to make amends?

And then there are the friendly strangers who show up on your Requests page. They may turn out to be wonderful people you're glad you've met, but they may also turn out to be creepy stalkers with no sense of boundaries. What to do?

As for your boss, see the *Facebook at Work* chapter for some perspective on that. For the strangers, see the "Stranger Danger" tip earlier in this chapter. And for the other head-scratchers, the advice is largely the same as for strangers:

1. Take your time to think it over.
2. Check out the relevant profiles.
3. Get input from mutual friends.

Once you've done all that, run the available data through that amazing biological computer known as your "gut," and see what answer you get.

Keep in mind that there may be less social cost to ignoring a friend request than to friending someone and then removing them later. As writer and BoingBoing blogger Cory Doctorow put it in an *InformationWeek* essay, "It's socially awkward to refuse to add someone to your Friends list—but removing someone from your Friends list is practically a declaration of war."

In the real world, skin comes in all degrees of thickness. One person may never notice that you ignored their friend request, while some other melodramatic soul takes it as a denial of their human worth.

You can't control other people's feelings, of course, or what molehills they mistake for mountains, and you have to do what's right for your own comfort and sanity. But it's also worth taking a moment to evaluate what you know of the person you're considering, how easily their feelings get hurt, and how much you care about keeping their good will.

One good rule of thumb for Facebook is that the less you know someone, the less you owe them. But it's also true that sometimes our best friends—and most valuable business contacts—are the ones we're just about to meet.

4

Privacy and Security

If you keep even half an eye on the news, you're aware that privacy and security are critically important issues online—and that's especially true in the social networking world. On sites like Facebook and MySpace, you can expose yourself to identity theft or fraud, just as with online shopping or banking sites. But on social networking sites, you also risk embarrassment or even censure if you wind up revealing the wrong details to the wrong people. Because you're on Facebook to make connections and share information, it can be easy to cross the line into revealing too much information. Sometimes it's hard to figure out where the line even is.

But don't panic. As long as you exercise a little caution, there's no reason the time you spend on Facebook should be any more perilous than a night on the town with friends. In both cases, it's important to keep your wits about you, know the lay of the land, and think before you share too much info with people you don't know very well.

In this chapter I'll give you tips on how to balance self-expression with discretion, and I'll explain the settings that Facebook provides to help you protect your privacy. But before we discuss Facebook's privacy and security tools, let's start by talking about the one you bring to the party yourself: your common sense.

🔒 Privacy

An Ounce of Discretion Is Worth a Ton of Privacy Settings

Most people have many different sides—and they often choose to share those sides with different sets of people. You might talk music with one set of friends who tend to share your taste, and sports with another set of friends. You might avoid talking politics or religion with certain friends because you know you don't see eye-to-eye with them.

But on Facebook, your friends will all see the same persona, consisting of whichever parts of your personality you use Facebook to express. Unless you use Facebook's privacy settings to carefully separate your social groups, as we'll discuss later in this chapter, friends with whom you don't normally discuss politics will see your political comments. Friends who have different taste in music from you might discover your passionate love of Barry Manilow or Night Ranger.

Family and friends mix together on Facebook, too. You may have friends with whom you tend to engage in salty repartee that you'd never want your mom to overhear, but if she's in your Facebook Friends list, she very well might.

There can also be academic and professional repercussions to how you express yourself on Facebook. Colleges have revoked admissions for students because of inappropriate postings on Facebook and MySpace, and employers increasingly check out the profiles of job candidates before making hiring decisions. Chatting about conditions at your current office can be a pitfall, too: If your boss is friends with anyone in the conversation, he or she could overhear the whole thing.

You shouldn't necessarily let those considerations stifle your self-expression on Facebook, but when you post, it might help to imagine that you're speaking to a large and diverse group at a party, rather than to a few intimate friends at your kitchen table.

It's true that using Facebook's privacy settings can provide some control over who sees what. But don't let those settings lull you into a false sense of security. Words and images posted on the Internet have a way of reaching a wider audience than originally intended, and once they do, trying to recall or erase them is like trying to put the proverbial toothpaste back in the tube. Or maybe more like trying to put Silly String back in the can.

The fact is, there's only one way to absolutely guarantee that a photo, video, or snatch of ribald banter won't be seen by more people than you want it to: Don't post it online in the first place.

Facebook's official privacy policy puts it this way: "Although we allow you to set privacy options that limit access to your pages, please be aware that no security measures are perfect or impenetrable. We cannot control the actions of other Users with whom you may choose to share your pages and information. Therefore, we cannot and do not guarantee that User Content you post on the Site will not be viewed by unauthorized persons."

In other words, Facebook's privacy and security tools can greatly *reduce* the chance that your information will be seen by the wrong eyes, but they can't rule it out entirely. You may be a Yoda-like master of Facebook's privacy settings (clicked all the checkboxes, you have!), but your info can still get away from you. For example, a trusted friend could easily fail to realize that a photo you posted was intended to be seen by only a very select audience, and might repost it somewhere else or e-mail it to a group of mutual friends—or people you don't even know.

Remember also that law enforcement officials can get a court order to view Facebook profile information. And I've heard one anecdotal account of a job seeker being asked by her prospective employers to log into Facebook and then leave the room while they reviewed her profile. If your potential bosses get to look at your profile the way you see it, privacy controls become irrelevant.

The bottom line is if you're truly worried that a bleary-eyed photo of you holding a plastic cup at a party could get you in trouble if it were seen by a prospective employer, an admissions board, or certain very conservative relatives, the safest approach is to simply not post it at all.

That doesn't mean you should censor yourself excessively or squelch every playful impulse. But you should consider the risks and benefits, and find a reasonable middle ground for self-expression that's within your personal comfort zone.

Friend Management: The Key to Choosing Your Audience

Unless you keep your Friends list small and exclusive, you'll find yourself friending and being befriended by more than just the dear old friends you'd trust with your house keys and your unlocked diary.

There will also be co-workers, casual acquaintances, friends of friends you met at a party, and old schoolmates you lost track of years ago, as well as all sorts of other gray-area cases. You may even be using Facebook to make friends with interesting new people you don't know very much about at all, just yet.

Fortunately, Facebook's Friend List feature (explained earlier in the *Friends* chapter) is a great tool for sorting and grouping your friends. And by organizing your friends according to your degree of intimacy with them, you can use your Friend Lists to filter how much and what you reveal to whom.

The Three-Level System

One simple system you can use is to sort your growing Facebook circle into three basic lists.

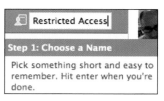

Creating a Trusted Friends list

Start by creating one list that's just for your nearest and dearest: the inner-circle friends who already know all your business, and whom you trust enough to grant total security clearance to your Facebook profile. Call this list something like Trusted Friends.

Next, create a second list for all the people in the middle. The people you don't know well enough to let them see you with your hair in curlers, or share your home address with, but also don't have any reason to feel wary of. Call this list something like Casual Friends or Acquaintances. This will probably be the biggest list and the one you add people to by default.

Finally, create a third list for people you don't know very well, aren't entirely sure how much you trust, or just want to keep an eye on until you have a better sense of what makes them tick. You can call this list something like Restricted Access or Watch List. (I call mine PIDRK, which stands for "People I Don't Really Know," but you might not find unwieldy acronyms as entertaining as I do.)

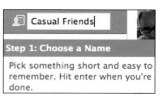

Creating a Casual Friends list

Once you've got those lists set up, it's time to perform a simple triage operation. Go through your All Friends list (choose Friends > All Friends in the blue bar), and assign everyone to one of those three lists.

Adding a friend to the Trusted Friends list

Click the triangle in the expanded entry for a friend to reveal a pop-up menu that will let you assign your friend to one of your lists.

Going forward, each time you add a new friend, you should automatically assign them to the appropriate list.

Here's another refinement: If you have family members whom you love and trust but still don't want seeing certain photos or comments you post, you might create a fourth list for them, called Family Members.

Once you get the hang of them, you can use Facebook's custom Friend Lists to sort your friends into as many different levels of security clearance as you want (up to Facebook's maximum of 100 lists), and as you'll see, there are lots of ways to put your custom lists to work.

Controlling Who Sees What

Facebook gives you some very specific settings for controlling what parts of your Facebook life are visible and who gets to see them.

Your home base for most of the settings you'll want to change is the Privacy Settings page. To find it, hover your pointer over Settings (at the top right of the screen, in the blue bar) until the menu appears. Then choose Privacy Settings.

Choose Privacy Settings from the Settings menu in the blue bar.

How to Customize Your Profile Info for Specific People

You can choose who has access to almost anything that appears on your Profile page. To start refining who sees which parts of your Facebook persona, Choose Settings > Privacy Settings > Profile, then choose the Basic tab.

The first control at the top of the page, labeled Profile, lets you choose who is allowed to visit your Facebook Profile page. Click the pop-up menu and you'll see four choices: My Networks and Friends, Friends of Friends, Only Friends, and Custom.

The menu choices for the Profile control

If you choose My Networks and Friends, then in addition to all of your Facebook friends, anyone who belongs to one of the Networks you've joined

NOTE: Clicking the Privacy link in the footer, down at the bottom of any Facebook page, doesn't take you to Facebook's Privacy settings—rather, it's how you access Facebook's privacy policy.

Friends of Friends

The theory behind the Friends of Friends option is that someone who shares a friend with you is part of your larger social circle, and someone you have a good chance of meeting socially. And at least one person you know made the decision to add this person as a friend, for whatever that's worth. Keep in mind, though, that sharing a mutual friend with you is not a guarantee that someone is trustworthy, because lots of people on Facebook make friends with people they don't know very well.

TIP: The controls for specific parts of your profile *override* the general Profile control at the top of the page. So, even if someone has access to your Profile page itself, if you've set the Personal Info control (for example) to hide that information from them, then it won't appear on the version of your Profile page they see. This allows you to pick and choose what people see, without shutting them out of your profile altogether.

can look at your Profile page. (This includes your regional Network, like Los Angeles; your school Networks; and your employer Networks.) This is the widest possible setting in terms of how many people you give access to—although it's still only a fraction of the total people on Facebook.

The next step down in visibility is the Friends of Friends option: Your profile will be open to all of your Facebook friends, *plus* any friend of one of your Facebook friends. It's more restrictive than the My Networks and Friends setting, because a person has to share at least one mutual friend with you before they can look at your Profile page.

The next setting, Only Friends, is fairly self-explanatory: Only people you've added as a friend on Facebook will be able to view your profile.

The fourth setting, Custom, opens the Edit Custom Settings dialog. The settings here are a little more complex but very useful, giving you more options for controlling who can see your information. If you want to slice up your profile information and serve different segments to different audiences, this is the place to do it.

The Edit Custom Settings dialog for the Profile control has three basic areas. The top area lets you choose which friends can view your information, the middle section lets you choose which Networks have access, and the bottom allows you to include or exclude certain categories of people.

There are specific controls for all the parts of your profile on the Privacy Settings > Profile page (under both the Basic and Contact Info tabs). Each control has its own pop-up menu, and they all work pretty much the same. To find out what a specific control like Status Updates affects, click on the little question mark next to the pop-up menu, and a description will appear.

How to Use Friend Lists to Fine-Tune Your Control

Here's one of the places where organizing your friends into Friend Lists really pays off. Some of the controls on the Privacy Settings > Profile page have additional options in the Custom dialog that let you choose specific Friend Lists to allow or deny access to.

For example, the Custom dialog for Status Updates has a Some Friends option in addition to Friends of Friends and Only Friends.

Choosing the Some Friends option in the Edit Custom Settings dialog for status updates opens up a field where you can type the names of specific friends or Friend Lists.

The Some Friends option is also available in the Custom dialogs for Photo Tagged of You, Videos Tagged of You, Wall Posts, Education Info, and Work Info, as well as all of the controls under the Contact Info tab.

So, for example, on the Contact Information tab you could choose a Friend List to share your mobile phone number with—so that only the people on that list have access to it. You might choose to display your work e-mail address only to the people on your Co-Workers Friend List, while sharing your personal address with the people on your Trusted Friends list.

Some of the controls also have an Except These People option down at the bottom of the Custom dialog.

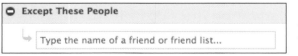

The Except These People option in the Edit Custom Settings dialog for status updates

This is where you get to put up the velvet rope that blocks access to specific parties. Anyone you enter in the Except These People field will be excluded from viewing the info in question, *regardless* of whether they belong to any of the categories, Friend Lists, or Networks you granted access to. You can type the names of individual people *or* Friend Lists in this field. If you already have a Friend List called Limited Profile or Restricted Access, you can enter it here.

TIP: The Networks you give access to in the Edit Custom Settings dialog are *in addition to* whatever you choose in the Friends area at the top of the dialog. So, for example, if you choose Only Friends, and then choose the Atlanta, GA Network in the Networks area, the total audience you've just given access to will equal the people you're friends with on Facebook *plus* anyone who belongs to the Atlanta, GA Network.

NOTE: When you're all done changing your settings on any of the Privacy Settings pages discussed in this section, you'll need to save your changes before they'll take effect—or you can cancel them. Thankfully, Facebook prompts you to save or cancel your changes before you click away from these pages, so you won't accidentally dump all the preferences you so carefully set up.

The controls on the "Actions within Facebook" tab let you choose what types of stories get published to your Wall and News Feed.

TIP: There is one checkbox I do recommend deselecting on the "Actions within Facebook" tab: Remove Profile Info. Facebook has an annoying tendency to report on tiny little tweaks you make to your profile info, and those stories aren't usually very interesting or useful to anyone. And really, what's the point of drawing attention to information you've chosen to remove?

NOTE: The "Show times in my Wall" checkbox adds a timestamp to each story, identifying at exactly what time the actions took place. Deselecting this checkbox will remove that timestamp from certain stories, but keep in mind that Wall posts and status updates always display the timestamp, regardless of this setting. So if you're trying to cover your tracks regarding exactly when you were goofing around on Facebook, this checkbox might not help all that much.

How to Control What Gets Announced on Your News Feed and Wall

A key part of the Facebook experience is that when you do certain things, Facebook announces it to your friends. If you add a new friend, post a photo or video, write on someone's Wall, or take other actions that might be interesting to your fans and admirers, Facebook may generate a story about it. (Examples: "Dave Awl is now friends with Becca Freed." Or "Dave Awl commented on Becca Freed's photo.") That story can then be visible to your Facebook friends in a variety of places, such as the News Feed area of the Home page.

The Privacy Settings > News Feed and Wall page lets you control whether or not Facebook generates those feed stories, and which ones.

The set of checkboxes under the heading "Actions visible to friends" is where you can allow or disallow specific kinds of stories. I recommend leaving most of these checkboxes selected, unless you're feeling incredibly shy or just aren't comfortable yet with Facebook's tendency to publicize what you do. (This "Facebook stage fright" is a fairly common reaction among Facebook newbies, but most people quickly become acclimated and recognize the value of letting their Facebook activities be visible.)

The "Show stories in Chat" option allows News Feed stories about you to be displayed within Facebook's Chat application. (See the *Communicating on Facebook* chapter for info on Chat.)

As Facebook makes explicitly clear on this page, there are certain actions that are never reported in Facebook stories. Here are the most important from the list: Inbox messages (which are private, as opposed to Wall posts); profiles, photos, and Notes that you view (Facebook doesn't report on your reading and browsing habits); and people you remove from your friends.

How to Control Whether You Show Up in Search Results

On the Privacy Settings page, click Search. You'll see a Search Discovery area with a Search Visibility pop-up menu.

The Search Visibility control

The default setting is Everyone, which means anyone who searches Facebook. (This doesn't mean they can see your profile—just the search result itself.) You can restrict your search visibility with the other choices in this menu, which work the same way as the Privacy controls already discussed.

The controls under the Search Result Content heading let you decide whether the people who aren't allowed to see your profile are able to contact you, and what forms of communication they can use.

The Public Search Listing control lets you decide whether people can find your Facebook listing on search engines such as Google, as well as within Facebook applications. Select the checkbox to create a public search listing, or deselect the checkbox if you don't want to make the listing available.

NOTE: The Public Search Listing control won't be available on your profile unless you choose Everyone from the Search Visibility menu. If you've chosen any of the more restrictive settings, the Public Search Listing control disappears from the page.

> **Public Search Listing**
>
> Use this setting to control what information is available outside of Facebook and when using applications.
>
> ☑ Create a public search listing for me and submit it for search engine indexing (see preview)

> **People who can see me in search can see:**
>
> ☑ My profile picture
> ☑ My friend list
> ☑ A link to add me as a friend
> ☑ A link to send me a message

The checkboxes that let you decide how people who can't see your profile can contact you

Click the "see preview" link to take a look at how your listing would appear, which may help you make up your mind.

NOTE: If you're a minor (meaning your age is listed on Facebook as under 18), no public search listing will be created for you, regardless of whether you select the public search listing checkbox.

How to Block People

If you don't want any contact with someone else who's on Facebook, you can block them on the Privacy Settings page. (This is an especially important step to perform if someone has harassed or threatened you in any way—right before you report that person to Facebook.)

Blocking someone on Facebook not only prevents them from using Facebook to contact or communicate with you on Facebook, it makes you virtually invisible to them—like Harry Potter's magic cloak.

TIP: Remember that the ability to look at your Friends list or send you an Inbox message may help a long-lost friend identify whether you're the person they used to know—or just someone with a similar name.

> **Block People**
>
> If you block someone, they will not be able to find you in a Facebook search, see your profile, or interact with you through Facebook channels (such as Wall posts, Poke, etc.). Any Facebook ties you currently have with a person you block will be broken (for example, friendship connections, Relationship Status, etc.). Note that blocking someone may not prevent all communications and interactions in third-party applications, and does not extend to elsewhere on the Internet.
>
> **Person**
>
> Uriah Heep   [**Block**]

To block someone, type his or her name in the box, and click Block. Facebook will show you a results page listing people who match what you typed, so that you can pick the precise person whom you want to block. Click Block Person next to the appropriate listing, and presto! You're done.

How to Opt Out of Appearing in Social Ads

Click the Social Ads tab on the Privacy Settings > News Feed and Wall page, and you'll arrive at the Social Ads page. If you buy something or become a fan of a Facebook Page after clicking on a Social Ad, then Facebook friends of yours may see your name and/or face appearing in that ad the next time it pops up for them.

You can opt out of appearing in Social Ads by setting the menu on the Social Ads page to "No one," instead of the default choice, "Only my friends." (See the *Pages and Ads* chapter for more about Social Ads.)

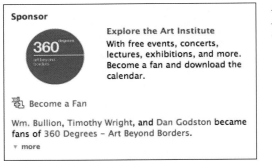

An example of a Social Ad showing the names of several friends

How to Opt Out of Beacon Advertising

Beacon is Facebook's advertising program that allows external Web sites to submit stories to your Facebook News Feed about purchases you make on those sites. For example, if you buy a movie ticket using Fandango, a message might appear on your Wall: "Harold Foo just bought a ticket to see *Wall-E* on Fandango."

Selecting the "Don't allow Beacon websites to post stories to my profile" checkbox on the Privacy Settings > Applications page opts you out of Beacon entirely, and no Beacon stories about you will be published on Facebook.

But even if you leave this box deselected, you'll still be given the opportunity to approve or cancel each individual Beacon story before it appears on your profile. So if you like sharing your taste in movies, music, or other purchases, you might prefer to leave this checkbox deselected, and then decide on a case-by-case basis whether you want any given story to appear. Approve the ones you like, and spike the ones you don't.

Keeping Applications in Line

Now that we've discussed the privacy settings for direct interaction with other people, let's talk about the settings for applications.

How to Authorize and Deauthorize Applications (and What Exactly That Means)

There's more detail about this in the *Applications and Other Add-Ons* chapter, but in a nutshell, applications aren't allowed to access most of your information until you *authorize* them. (This usually happens the first time you use an application, when you click the Allow button in the dialog that gives you access to it.)

You can authorize and deauthorize applications on the Applications page, which you can get to by choosing Application Settings from the Settings menu in the blue bar.

> **NOTE:** Once you do authorize an application, it can access any of the information that's available on your profile, with the important exception of your contact info. Also, applications are required to respect your privacy settings when accessing your profile info.

Application Settings – Authorized

Displaying 184 applications you have authorized.   Show: | Authorized ▼ |

▼ **Applications on Facebook**

G **(Lil) Green Patch**		Edit Settings	About	X
🦍 **(fluff)Friends**		Edit Settings	About	X
⏱ **10 Second Interview**		Edit Settings	About	X
ᴬᴰ **Addicted to Arrested Development**		Edit Settings	About	X
▮ **Addicted to Doctor Who**		Edit Settings	About	X

- Choosing Authorized from the menu at the top of the Applications page lets you see which applications are currently authorized. Clicking the X on the right side of the entry for an application will allow you to remove (deauthorize) that application, or completely block the application if you so choose.
- Choosing Allowed to Post from the menu shows you which applications are currently allowed to publish stories to your News Feed (such as, "Dave Awl just sent a Knight who says 'Ni!' to a friend using Monty Python Gifts"). Click the Edit Settings link next to an application to edit its posting permissions.

■ Choosing Granted Additional Permissions from the menu will show you the applications that are allowed to access your information even when you're not online, as well as the applications that are allowed to send you notifications by e-mail. Click the Edit Settings link to make changes.

How to Keep Applications You Don't Use from Accessing Your Information

The Privacy Settings > Applications > Settings page lets you limit what information friends can see about you when they're using an application you don't use yourself.

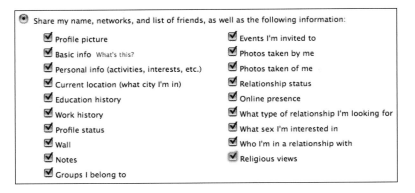

By selecting or deselecting these checkboxes, you can choose to make such info as your education history, your photos, or whether you're online or not (just to pick a few examples) off-limits to applications you haven't authorized.

There's a clear trade-off here: The more of these checkboxes you deselect, the more you protect your privacy—but the less your friends will be able to interact and communicate with you using applications on Facebook. (For example, they might be prevented from sending you a message or a gift, or dedicating a song to you, from their favorite application.)

It's a little like making your phone number unlisted—it protects you from bill collectors and crank callers, but it may also make it harder for the people you actually like to give you a jingle.

How to Block Applications You Don't Want to Deal With

Each request you receive from an application is accompanied by a Block This Application link. Clicking Block This Application prevents persistently annoying applications from contacting you or accessing your information.

The Blocked Applications area on the Privacy Settings > Applications > Settings page shows a listing of all applications you've blocked so far. You can click the "remove" link next to an application's name to take it off the blacklist.

 TIP: You can also block specific applications from the main Applications page.

How to Block Application Requests from Specific People

Just as you can block applications you don't like, you can also choose to ignore all invites from particular friends who send you requests you're not interested in. Each request is accompanied by an Ignore All Invites From This Friend link. Clicking it means that in the future you won't receive any requests from that friend.

Any friends you've chosen to ignore invites from will be listed on the Privacy Settings > Applications > Settings page. You can click the "remove" link next to any person to take them off this list and restore their ability to send you application requests.

Facebook Security 101

Here are some basic tips for a safer and more secure Facebook experience. These are mostly common sense, but even if you're a veteran Facebooker, it doesn't hurt to be reminded of them.

- Choose a secure password for your Facebook account (one that uses both numbers and letters, isn't a word that can be found in a dictionary, and isn't something anyone else could guess) and *never* share your password with anyone else.
- Be careful about whom you friend. See the "Stranger Danger" and "To Friend or Not to Friend" sidebars in the *Friends* chapter for some perspective on this. And remember that online, people aren't always who they seem to be.
- Be suspicious of links to external sites, and don't enter your passwords or other sensitive info unless you're certain the site you're on is legitimate.
- If someone uses Facebook to threaten or harass you, report them to Facebook immediately.

 Privacy Settings for Photos and Videos
You can edit privacy settings for photo albums or videos on the Edit Info page for the album or video in question. As with applications and the various information on your profile, you can use Networks and Friend Lists to specify exactly who you do and don't want to see what you've posted. See the *Photos and Videos* chapter for full details on creating and editing photo albums and videos.

WARNING: If you use a shared computer or access Facebook from a public space, make sure to deselect the Remember Me checkbox when you log in to Facebook. And don't forget to log out when you finish your Facebook session. Otherwise you may wind up giving the next person to use the computer complete access to your Facebook account.

Reporting Abuse

If you see hateful, abusive, or otherwise objectionable content that violates Facebook's Terms of Use, you can report it anonymously to Facebook.

You can also anonymously report individuals who post offensive content, or who harass or threaten you or any other Facebook users.

Facebook will investigate, and if the complaint is legitimate, Facebook will take the appropriate steps to warn or remove the parties responsible.

If you spot a profile with objectionable content, you can click the Report This Person link toward the bottom of the profile to send a report to Facebook. (Note that you won't see this link if you're friends with the person in question. If you're actually going to report on a friend, you'd probably want to defriend that person first anyway.)

Facebook Groups have a similar link (Report Group) on their pages that you can use to report objectionable Groups, and so do Photos and Notes. You can report individual Wall posts and other messages using the Report link underneath each posting.

Finally, if you can't find a Report link, you can always send an e-mail message to *abuse@facebook.com* to notify Facebook of objectionable content or behavior. You can even report objectionable ads to Facebook, if you see any, by e-mailing *advertise@facebook.com*. Facebook says it will "use [its] best efforts" to remove ads that violate its terms of use.

Phishing

The term *phishing* refers to a kind of online fraud in which criminals try to trick people into revealing their passwords, credit card numbers, and other sensitive data.

You may already be familiar with phishing e-mails, which are spam messages disguised to look like e-mail from your bank or other sites you do business with, such as PayPal and eBay. Clicking a link in a phishing e-mail takes you to a fake site that's mocked up to look like the real thing, where the phishers hope you'll trustingly enter your information.

You can often identify phishing e-mails because they don't address you by your real name the way your bank would, or because they're littered with typos and bad grammar. (For some reason that escapes me, highly literate people rarely seem to choose phishing as a career path.) Threats are another giveaway—phishing e-mails often claim that dire consequences will occur if

What's "Objectionable"?
Obviously, deciding what's objectionable can be subjective, but Facebook's terms of use expressly prohibit nudity, pornography, harassment, and unwelcome contact. Objectionable content, according to Facebook, includes "content that *we deem* to be harmful, threatening, unlawful, defamatory, infringing, abusive, inflammatory, harassing, vulgar, obscene, fraudulent, invasive of privacy or publicity rights, hateful, or racially, ethnically or otherwise objectionable." In other words, the definition of *objectionable* is ultimately up to Facebook's judgment.

you don't do what's requested. It's all just an attempt to intimidate you into clicking that bogus link.

On Facebook, phishing commonly takes the form of a message or Wall posting that *appears* to come from someone on your Friend List—but in reality, your friend's account has been compromised, and the message has been sent by scamsters using the login information they stole from your friend. The phishers are hoping you'll trust the message because you trust your friend, and click the link and enter your information before you have time to realize that the message is, well, phishy. If you take the bait, and the phishers gain access to your own user name and password, very shortly your other friends will start to get phishing messages that appear to come from you.

What Phishing Looks Like

If you see a posting like this appear on your Wall, you'll know the friend who supposedly posted it got phished.

Note the telltale signs of a dodgy post: the all caps, the bad punctuation and spelling. And of course, the most important clue of all—the whole point of the post is to get you to visit a spammy Web site, which is no doubt crawling with viruses, malware, and other nastiness.

Phighting Back: Tips for Not Getting Phished

Phishing is common enough on Facebook that sooner or later you'll come across it, if you haven't already.

Education is your best weapon against phishers—once you know how phishing works, you're less likely to take the bait. So here's a bucketful of tips to help you keep from getting phished:

- Make sure your browser is up to date and secure. Current browsers are getting better at identifying and warning you about suspicious sites. Make sure you've got the most up-to-date version of whatever browser you're using.

Become a Fan of Facebook Security

The Facebook Security Page is a good central resource for information about phishing, viruses, and other security topics. You can find it easily by typing *Facebook Security* into Facebook's search box.

By clicking the Become a Fan link in the upper-right area of the page, you'll be signed up for updates from Facebook related to security and safety topics. (And your News Feed will most likely mention that you've become a fan of Facebook Security, helping to spread the word about this resource to your friends. One good deed for the day done!)

■ Don't click any links, especially links to external Web sites, if you're not sure where they go. And pay attention to the URL in your browser. Mouse over the link before you click it, and look at the URL that appears in the status bar of your browser. If it doesn't match the address the link is supposed to take you to, that's a reason to be suspicious.

■ Be suspicious of any Wall posts or messages that don't sound like the friend who supposedly wrote them. If the grammar, spelling, or syntax isn't what you'd expect from the person you know, that's a red flag.

■ Set up a security question for your Facebook account. If phishers do manage to take control of it, Facebook's User Operations team can help you restore your access by having you provide the answer to your security question. (You can set your security question on the Settings > Account Settings page.)

■ Remember that Facebook will never ask you to provide your password in an e-mail or Inbox message.

■ Help police Facebook by watching your friends' backs—if it looks like a friend of yours has been phished, let them know immediately.

TIP: One caveat regarding security questions: Make sure the answer to your question isn't something that anyone else could guess or discover from publicly available information. If someone can find out the name of your pet by Googling your name, for example, then don't use the name of your pet.

What to Do If You Get Phished

If you discover that your Facebook account has been accessed by phishers, there are three steps to take immediately.

1. **Reset your password** on the Settings > Account Settings page. (As mentioned earlier, if your login information no longer works, you may need to provide Facebook with the answer to your security question so they can restore access to your account.)

2. **Report abuse to Facebook.** Click the Help link in the footer on any Facebook page. Then type the words *report phishing* in the search box for a link to the form where you can submit a phishing report to Facebook.

3. **Run antivirus software** to check your computer for any malware you may have picked up.

Beware of Links Bearing Trojans

Phishing isn't the only reason to be careful where you click on Facebook. At the time of this writing, there's a virus (technically a worm delivered by means of a Trojan horse) called Koobface that's spreading via Inbox message spam on Facebook.

If you get one of these messages—which may appear to come from a friend whose computer has been infected—you'll see a link to an online video player. Once you're on the video page, a message tells you that you won't be able to play the video without downloading an upgrade to your video software. But if you click the link, you'll wind up downloading the Trojan and potentially infecting your own computer.

I've seen this one in action myself. One morning not too long ago, I woke up and logged onto Facebook to find a message in my Inbox from an old college friend. It was just a one-sentence message, of the "Hey, look at this" variety, with a link.

I was still half asleep and not thinking suspiciously, so I clicked the link. (Only later, when I was little more awake, did it occur to me that the friend in question almost never sent me messages littered with misspellings, smileys, and LOLs.)

After clicking, here's what I saw:

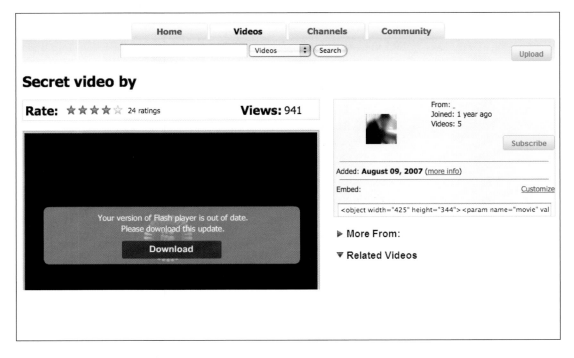

Fortunately, I'd read about this particular Trojan, so I knew enough not to download the bogus video software. And now you do, too.

If You're Under 18

If you're legally a minor—or if you have family members who are minors using Facebook—you need to pay extra attention, and give extra weight, to the security warnings and safety tips in this chapter.

The sobering reality is that people online are not always who they pretend to be, and predators do use the Internet to stalk and "groom" underage victims. Online bullying is also a sad reality, and people have been known to assume false identities for this purpose.

Facebook does its best to identify fake profiles and shut them down—and in fact has sometimes taken criticism for being too aggressive in its approach. But Facebook's security team isn't omniscient, and despite its efforts, fake profiles do get created and do get used for some dishonorable purposes.

In addition to the general security and safety tips shared elsewhere in this chapter, minors on Facebook should take these precautions:.

- Don't post your address or phone number online, anywhere. Don't trust Facebook's privacy settings to limit access to them. Let e-mail be your first point of contact for anyone who doesn't already have your number.
- Don't friend anyone you don't already know and trust.
- Make sure you familiarize yourself with Facebook's privacy settings, and set them carefully. Check them every so often to make sure you're still comfortable with the level of privacy you've chosen.
- Don't arrange to meet anyone offline for the first time without other people you know and trust being present and knowing in advance about the meeting.
- Don't feel obligated to post an actual photo of yourself as your main profile pic. Your profile picture can show up in all sorts of places on Facebook other than your profile itself (including search listings, Groups, third-party apps, and more), so it may be seen by people you aren't friends with. Lots of people on Facebook use an avatar other than their own photo—such as an image of a pet, a favorite possession, or even an illustration—that says something about them but doesn't compromise their privacy.
- Block anyone who sends you inappropriate communications (see the info on how to block people earlier in this chapter) and report them to Facebook (see "Reporting Abuse"). And as Facebook says on its Safety page, "We strongly encourage users under the age of 18 to talk to their parents or a responsible adult immediately if someone online says or does something to make them feel uncomfortable or threatened in any way."

Keeping a Low Profile

Lurking is a time-honored tradition on the Internet. Some people are shy. Others need to fly under the radar for reasons related to their careers or personal lives.

If you're one of those people, you may wonder whether it's possible to lurk quietly on Facebook at all, given that Facebook's default approach is to announce what people do.

But it is possible to keep a low profile on Facebook, by setting your privacy controls to the maximum and declining to post any personal info on your profile.

Once you've followed the steps below, nobody you haven't explicitly chosen to be friends with on Facebook will be able to tell you're on Facebook at all. And even your friends won't see much information about you, if any. You can lurk to your heart's content.

Of course, you'll be missing out on most of the fun of Facebook, which is about interaction, after all—but fortunately, all of the steps are reversible if and when you decide to come out of your shell.

So here's your step-by-step guide to Facebooking on the down-low:

1. Set your profile visibility to Only Friends (the narrowest possible setting) on the Privacy Settings > Profile page.

2. You may also want to delete personal info from your profile, using the Edit My Profile link on your Profile page, if you've entered any. The only info you can't erase from your profile is your name. Everything else—your hometown, your birthday, even your gender—is optional.

3. Set Search Visibility to Only Friends (the narrowest possible setting) on the Privacy Settings > Search page. (This will also cause the Public Search Listing checkbox to disappear, and remove your public search listing, if you had one.)

4. In the Search Result Content settings on the Privacy Settings > Search page, deselect all of the checkboxes, so people you aren't friends with can't contact you, friend you, or view your picture or Friends list.

5. On the Privacy Settings > News Feed and Wall page, deselect all check-boxes under "Actions Visible to Friends."

6. On the Applications page, deauthorize all applications.

7. Leave any networks you've joined. You can do this by visiting the Settings > Account Settings > Networks page.

WARNING: One thing I *don't* recommend you do is use a pseudonym on Facebook—that's a violation of Facebook's Terms of Use and can get you permanently banned. (See the *Signing Up and Setting Up Your Profile* chapter.)

Quitting Facebook

Some people resist joining Facebook precisely because of the popular misconception that once you set up a Facebook profile, you can never remove your information. I have one friend who starts singing the lyrics from "Hotel California" (*you can check out any time you like/but you can never leave*) anytime the word Facebook is mentioned.

So in case you're afraid of being assigned a permanent residence at the Hotel Facebook (and having an Eagles song stuck in your head for all eternity), I'm going to tell you exactly how to pack up and leave Facebook if you ever decide you need to.

There's usually a kernel of truth behind any popular misconception. And in this case it's true that, technically speaking, you can't expunge your Facebook profile itself without going to the trouble of contacting Facebook and waiting for them to get around to complying with your request.

But it doesn't necessarily matter. Because what you *can* do anytime you want is delete any and all of the information in your profile, leaving a blank space behind where it used to be. And then you can cause your profile to disappear from search listings, so that nobody can find their way to the empty husk that used to hold your information. At which point, who cares if the hollowed-out profile itself is still sitting on Facebook's servers?

There are basically three ways to leave Facebook:

NOTE: If you choose temporary deactivation, you can reactivate your account at any time by logging in to Facebook with your e-mail and password.

TIP: While you're deactivated your friends will no longer see you in their Friends lists. You might want to let them know you're deactivating, so that they don't think you've defriended them.

1. **Deactivating temporarily.** If you choose this option, you'll vanish from Facebook for the time being, but the door will be open if you want to come back at some point in the future.

   To temporarily deactivate your Facebook account: Go to Settings > Account Settings and click the Deactivate link. Fill out the form letting Facebook know why you're deactivating, and then click the Deactivate button to confirm.

2. **Permanently deleting your account.** If you choose this option, you'll be submitting a request to Facebook to permanently remove your profile from Facebook. This step is not reversible (that's why it's called "permanent").

   To erase your Facebook account forever, click Help in the footer, and then type *Delete* in the Help Center's search field. Click "I want to permanently delete my account" on the results page, read the instructions, and click the link to the Delete Account form.

3. **The manual scrub.** If you really want to remove all your traces from Facebook, you can delete all of your profile info yourself before you

submit your deactivation or deletion request, and set all of your privacy controls to the max as described earlier in the "Keeping a Low Profile" section.

This step isn't technically necessary, but it might give you some extra satisfaction to know that all of your data has been wiped away before you shut down your profile. And it won't matter if it takes Facebook a while to process your permanent removal, because you'll know your information is already gone.

Once you've cleaned up your campsite, you can go ahead and choose permanent deletion as described in option 2.

Confirm Facebook Account Deactivation

Please let us know why you are deactivating. (required)

○ I don't find Facebook useful.

○ I don't understand how to use the site.

○ Facebook is resulting in social drama for me.

○ I need to fix something in my account.

○ I receive too many emails from Facebook.

○ I don't feel safe on the site.

○ I have another Facebook account.

○ I spend too much time using Facebook.

○ This is temporary. I'll be back.

○ Other

Please explain further:

The options on the Account Deactivation form let you tell Facebook why you're leaving. Or if you know it's only temporary, you can click the second-to-last option to let Facebook know you'll be back.

Delete My Account

If you do not think you will use Facebook again and would like your account deleted, we can take care of this for you. Keep in mind that you will not be able to reactivate your account or retrieve any of the content or information you have added. If you would like your account deleted, then click "Submit."

[Submit]   [Cancel]

The dialog for deleting your account warns you that this step is permanent.

5

Wall, Status, and News Feeds

Here's where the fun of Facebook truly begins. Spiffing up your profile and collecting friends is all well and good, but the secret ingredient to Facebook's success is the way it keeps you connected to your friends, making it easy to share news, info, and photos with each other.

Before Facebook came along, you might have dug up old friends on the Internet whom you hadn't seen in years, and swapped an excited e-mail or two in an attempt to catch up. But unless you really *worked* at keeping in contact, all too often you'd find that within six months or a year you'd fallen out of touch again.

Fortunately, Facebook takes the heavy lifting out of staying connected. Facebook's profiles give you an easy way to check in on any specific friends to see what they've been up to lately, while the News Feed that appears on your Home page give you a big-picture briefing on what's going on with your social circle from day to day and week to week.

In this chapter, we'll explore how all of that works. Plus, we'll talk about how you can use Facebook as a promotional tool: If you have something you'd like to spread the word about, Facebook's News Feeds can amplify your message and help you reach more people more effectively.

Facebook Publisher:
One-Stop Posting and Sharing

Up at the top of the Wall tab on your profile lives a special area, which (although it isn't labeled as such) is called the Facebook Publisher. The Publisher makes it easy to post all sorts of content to your profile: messages, links, photos, videos, and more. You can also use the Publisher on your friends' profiles to post content to their Walls.

Jane Musser

| Wall | Info | Photos | **+** |

👤 Update Status   📑 Share Link   📷 Add Photos   🎥 Add Video   ☐ Write Note   ▼

What are you doing right now? | **Post** |

TIP: If you don't see the button you're looking for along the top of the Publisher, just click the triangle button on the right side for a pop-up menu with more choices. The buttons for basic Facebook apps and functions are always available in the Publisher (including Notes, Posted Items, Photos, Videos, Import, and Write), but buttons for recently used apps can appear there as well, which causes the order of the buttons to shift around. So whatever there isn't room for above the Publisher gets shifted to the pop-up menu as overflow.

What does it mean to post something to your profile? (Wow, you ask the best questions.) As a matter of fact, there are two things happening at once.

First of all, when you post something to your profile, you're posting it on your Wall—a story about the item will appear among the other stories on your Wall, and friends who drop by your profile to check out what you've been up to will see it there.

But you're also engaging in a kind of targeted broadcasting. Facebook will generate a News Feed story about the item you've posted, which your friends may see the next time they look at the News Feed area on their Home pages. So when you post an item to your profile, you're also sharing it with your friends—saying, in effect, "Hey, everyone—look at this!"

To post something using the Publisher, click the button for the type of item you want to post (if it isn't already selected). This will cause the appropriate fields and controls to appear.

👤 **Update Status**   📑 Share Link   📷 Add Photos   🎥 Add Video   ☐ Write Note   💬 Write   📶 Import

The buttons for Facebook's basic applications and functions are available either above the Publisher or in the pop-up menu.

We'll look at the specifics of posting Wall messages, status updates, links, and Notes in the course of this chapter. Photos and videos are discussed in the *Photos and Videos* chapter.

Wall Basics

The Wall tab on the Profile page is where a big chunk of the direct, person-to-person social interaction on Facebook takes place. It's where you and your friends can leave each other social messages that other friends are allowed to see, and the place you drop by to see what's going on in the brain of any particular friend you'd like to catch up with.

How to Post to a Wall

Taking It Private
Wall posts, by design, are public conversations—like talking to a friend at a party where the other people gathered around can hear. But if you want to talk privately with a friend on Facebook, you can do that, too, by sending them an Inbox message or by using Facebook's Chat application. Both are discussed in detail in the following chapter, *Communicating on Facebook*.

Writing on someone's Wall is easy. Just go to their profile and click the Write button on the Publisher. Type your message in the field that appears, and click the Post button when you're done.

In addition to writing messages, you can use the Publisher to post links, photos, or videos on your friends' Walls—all the same kinds of items you can post to your own profile. Just choose the appropriate button on the Publisher.

Viewing Wall-to-Wall Conversations

Wall conversations can be fragmented by nature. A friend writes a message on your Wall, and you write a response on your friend's Wall, and so on. It's a complete conversation, but its two halves are in two different places. And if the conversation is spread out over several days, or even weeks, things become even more disjointed.

Can You Write on Your Own Wall?
Facebook gives you the option of writing a message on your own Wall, and there are times when you might have the urge to do that. For example, if someone asks you a question on your Wall, and the answer might be of interest to lots of your friends, you might want to post your answer where everyone in your Friends list can see it. But in that case, it might make even more sense to write a Note, so you can take advantage of the Notes application's tagging and formatting features. See the section "Notes: Blogging on Facebook," later in this chapter, for details.

Fortunately, Facebook gives you an easy way to read the whole conversation in one place, so you don't have to keep clicking back and forth between the two Walls in order to refresh your memory about what's already been said. At the bottom of any message someone writes on your Wall, you'll see a link that says Wall-to-Wall. (This doesn't include comments on News Feed stories that appear on your Wall; only freestanding Wall posts have Wall-to-Wall links.)

Matt Solomon wrote at 1:01pm
i think i have all the magazines too, but i have to dig 'em out. not nearly as good as the comics.

did you see steve gerber passed away earlier this year?
Wall-to-Wall · Write on Matt's Wall

Clicking the Wall-to-Wall link takes you to a page where you can see all the Wall messages between you and the friend in question.

> **My Wall–to–Wall with Matt Solomon**
> Back to My Profile
>
> Write something...
>
> 🎁 Give a Gift to Matt   Post
>
> **Matt Solomon (Madison, WI) wrote**
> at 1:01pm
> i think i have all the magazines too, but i have to dig 'em out. not nearly as good as the comics.
>
> did you see steve gerber passed away earlier this year?
> Write on Matt's Wall – Delete
>
> **Dave Awl wrote**
> at 8:28pm yesterday
> Hey, I just finally got around to ordering The Essential HTD from Amazon ... thanks again for the pointer on that. Waugh!

The Wall-to-Wall view lets you see all the back-and-forth between you and a specific friend, and also lets you post your next message on their Wall.

You may also see Wall-to-Wall links underneath stories that appear in your News Feed when one of your friends writes on another friend's Wall. This "third party" Wall-to-Wall view is especially useful, because a single Wall post by itself might not make much sense, but by clicking the Wall-to-Wall view you can get the context necessary to follow the conversation.

TIP: You can also control which (if any) applications are allowed to post stories to your Wall, using the settings on the Applications page. See the *Privacy and Security* chapter for details.

NOTE: The Wall-to-Wall view won't be available unless you're friends with both parties to the conversation—or allowed to view both parties' Walls because you fall within their chosen privacy settings.

Care and Feeding of Your Wall

Facebook gives you a fairly generous amount of control over what appears on your Wall—it's your place, after all.

How to Edit Wall Stories

For each story that appears on your Wall, you have the option to control the size of the story (how detailed it is) or delete it altogether. To edit a story, move your pointer over the right side of it until the Edit control appears.

> 🎐 Dave became a fan of Studs Terkel. 3:43am - Comment   Edit ✏️

The Edit control appears when you mouse over the right side of a Wall story.

Click the word Edit or the Pencil icon, and you'll see a menu of whatever options are available for that story. For some stories, Delete will be the only

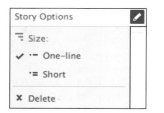

The pop-up menu for a Wall story may include size choices in addition to the option to delete it.

option—but if the story is available in different sizes, you can choose from One-line, Short, and in some cases Full.

Dave became a fan of Studs Terkel. 3:43am

Writer
2,735 fans

Add Comment

Changing the story size from One-line to Short allowed this story to appear in its expanded form, which includes a photo.

How to Control Who Can Post on Your Wall and See What's Posted There

☑ Friends may post to my Wall

🔒 Who can see posts made by friends?

Custom

👥 Only Friends
🖼 Neo-Futurists

Edit Custom Settings

The Wall Settings include a control that lets you choose whether friends can post to your Wall and who can see what gets posted.

As you might remember from the *Privacy and Security* chapter, there's a control on the Settings > Privacy Settings > Profile page that lets you choose whether or not your friends can post to your Wall. It also lets you specify who can view what your friends post, by choosing from your Networks or Friend Lists. You'll find that this same control is also available in the Settings area for your Wall. Click the Settings link at the top of your Wall, just under the Publisher, to display the Settings area.

All Posts   Posts by Dave   Posts by Others   ⚙ Settings

The controls at the top of the Wall tab, just underneath the Publisher, let you change views and also access settings for the Wall.

How to Change Your Wall's View

Along the top of your Wall you'll find a set of links that let you change what's displayed on your Wall. The default setting is All Posts, but if you click "Posts by *Your Name*" the view will change to show you only what you've posted to your profile yourself. Clicking "Posts by Others" shows you only what your friends have posted to your Wall.

Note that when you click these links, you're not actually removing or deleting anything from your Wall, and you're not hiding anything from other visitors to your Wall—you're just temporarily changing what's displayed to you.

The same view options are available when you're reading your friends' Walls, too. So if you're visiting Tracey's Wall, for example, you can click "Posts by Tracey" to see only what Tracey herself has posted, or "Posts by Others" to see what Tracey's friends have contributed to her Wall.

Feeding Frenzy: Using Feeds to Keep Track of Your Friends

I've said earlier that Facebook makes it easy to stay on top of what's going on with your friends, and the News Feed area on Facebook's Home page is where that happens. (See the "Social Section" sidebar at right for an explanation of what it's all about.) Facebook gives you some useful options for changing what kinds of stories you see in the News Feed, and homing in on stories featuring the friends you're most interested in.

How to Change the Display for the News Feed

Running along the top of the News Feed area on the Home page are four tabs. Clicking them lets you choose what kinds of stories you see.

- **News Feed** is the default view—think of it as a kind of "Facebook Digest." Facebook automatically analyzes a number of factors (including what kinds of stories and whose profiles you've clicked on recently) and then chooses a handful of stories it thinks you'll be interested in.
- **Status Updates, Photos,** and **Posted Items** each filter the view to show you only that kind of item.
- **Live Feed** is the raw, unfiltered experience—all of the News Feed stories about your friends appear here in chronological order. If you have a lot of friends, you might not be able to read through it all, but clicking on it occasionally gives you a level of detail—and some interesting surprises, sometimes—that you won't get from the News Feed (default) tab.

To the right of the tabs is a triangle button with a pop-up menu that gives you even more options. The top area lets you choose to see stories related to a specific app, while the bottom area lets you choose one of your Friend Lists.

TIP: This is the option I find most useful. If you've got a lot of Facebook friends, it can be a huge time commitment to try to keep up with all of the stories the News Feed provides. But you can easily create a Friend List called Favorites, and then choose that from the triangle button menu, to make it easy to stay briefed on the friends you're most interested in. You might also use this option to prioritize news about family, or business colleagues, or old friends you've just reconnected with and whose lives you're catching up on. All you have to do is create the corresponding Friend List, and it'll appear in the News Feed's menu the next time you load the Home page.

The Social Section

Imagine that you're reading the morning news on a Web portal where your news is arranged into sections. You click on the World tab for your international stories, the Tech tab for computer-related news, the Entertainment tab for movie and music news, and the Sports tab to keep track of your teams.

Now imagine that there's a tab there called Friends, and when you click on it, you get updates about what's going on in your personal social sphere. You might find out that two of your friends have gotten engaged and that several others are going to a concert this weekend. You might also read a political rant by your friend Kevin and some philosophical musings by Maria, and then see some freshly taken photos of Kurt's trip to Germany.

That's basically how the News Feed on Facebook's Home page works. If you make a habit of visiting the Home page on a regular basis, Facebook will gradually catch you up on all the developments—big and small—that your friends choose to share on Facebook.

The News Feed may also allow you to see sides of your friends that you haven't seen before. You might discover that a co-worker with whom you've never talked music has a collection of vintage rockabilly LPs that rivals your own, or that an old friend from college now makes beautiful hand-designed jewelry that she sells at craft shows on the weekends.

In addition to the controls on the Options for News Feed page, individual News Feed stories on the Home page have a Pencil icon that appears when you mouse over them. Click the Pencil icon to give Facebook feedback on how often you'd like to see certain kinds of stories, or stories about specific friends.

The Options for News Feed link lives at the bottom of the Home page, just above the footer.

TIP: If you don't recognize what the various icons above the sliders mean, just mouse over them and a label will appear for each slider.

Type the names of friends you'd like to see stories about more often.

TIP: Click the Remove link next to any name to remove that person from the More/Less About These Friends list.

How to Control What Stories Appear in the News Feed

Way down at the bottom of the News Feed area on the Home page is a link that's easy to overlook: Options for News Feed. Clicking it takes you to a page of controls that let you choose what kinds of News Feed stories you're interested in seeing, and which friends you'd like to see stories about most often.

At the top of the page you'll see a set of slider controls. Set the sliders higher for the kinds of stories you're most interested in, and lower for the ones you don't care so much about.

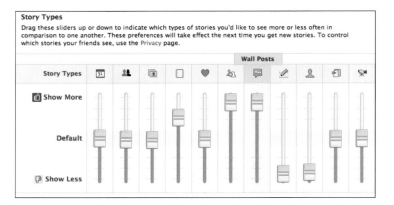

Down at the bottom is an area labeled More About These Friends, where you can enter the names of friends you're very interested in, and Facebook will prioritize stories about those people in your News Feed. To the right of that is the corresponding Less About These Friends area, where you can enter the names of people you're not so interested in, and Facebook will show you less stories about those friends.

How to Subscribe to News About Your Friends Using RSS

If you use an RSS reader, like Google Reader or Bloglines, you can use it to keep track of friends you're particularly interested in by subscribing to their Facebook News Feeds.

SUBSCRIBING TO STATUS UPDATES

You can subscribe to your friends' status updates by clicking Friends in the blue bar and then clicking the Status Updates tab at the top of the page. On the next page, look for the button that says Friends' Status Feed. Clicking that will give you the RSS feed link that you can enter into your RSS reader or browser.

SUBSCRIBING TO POSTED ITEMS

You can also subscribe to your friends' Posted Items—either for all your friends collectively or for any specific friend. To do this, go to the Posted Items application and look for the My Friends' Posted Items button. Clicking that will give you the link for the RSS feed.

To subscribe to Posted Items for a specific friend, first choose their name from the pop-up menu at the top of the Posted Items page. Then click the button that says *Your Friend's* Posted Items.

SUBSCRIBING TO NOTES

This works exactly like the process for Posted Items above—go to the Notes application, and look for the RSS link for your friends' Notes, or any specific friend's Notes, by choosing their name from the pop-up menu at the top.

The Tao of Status Updates

Once your Friends list grows to a significant size—by the time your friends number in the several dozens, say—reading status updates becomes not only a form of entertainment, but a surprisingly useful way to learn things. Clicking on the Status Updates tab on the Home page can feel like you're accessing the collective psyche of your social sphere, the *zeitgeist* of your Friends list—only instead of the spirit of an age you're tapping into, it's the spirit of a particular morning, afternoon, or evening.

If you're new to Facebook, I highly recommend getting in the habit of checking your friends' status updates on a regular basis. You may be surprised at some of the things you learn. For one thing, status updates can alert you to interesting trends among the people you know. You might discover that an alarming number of your friends are coming down with colds or sniffles (note to self: stock up on zinc lozenges!), or that a bunch of them are excited about the new season of *Mad Men*, or that several are heading to a nearby state to volunteer for flood relief work.

I'm amazed at how often I first hear about breaking news events on Facebook. Barack Obama's victory in the 2008 Iowa caucuses, the deaths of Heath Ledger and George Carlin, earthquakes in California and Illinois—these are all news events I learned about from reading my friends' status updates before clicking over to Google News for the full details. And the day I found out that several of my friends had been laid off from different employers in the same afternoon served as a local, human counterpoint to reading about unemployment figures in the news.

The button for subscribing to your friends' status updates via RSS on the Friends page

TIP: Each Friend List you create has its own specific feed for status updates—so if you want to subscribe to updates from just your close friends, for example, you could choose your Trusted Friends list. Select the list you're interested in from the list on the left of the Friends page, and then look for the Friends' Status Updates button on the Status Updates page for that list.

The button for subscribing to your friends' Posted Items (above) and the button for a specific friend's Posted Items (below)

TIP: While we're on the subject of feeds: You can also subscribe to your Facebook Notifications via RSS. Just go to your Notifications page (click Inbox in the blue bar and then choose the Notifications tab) and look for the Subscribe to Notifications button.

Ways to Use Your Status Update

Status updates are an interesting medium, because despite their brevity—they generally allow for only one or two sentences at most—you can use them to say so many different types of things.

Status updates can serve as a personal journal, in which you record the little details and experiences of your day; a standup comic's microphone, where you crack jokes and serve up wry observations; or an activist's megaphone that lets you disseminate information and share your perspective on current issues and events. Most likely, your status updates will be a mix of all of those different modes, and more.

You can also use your status updates as a promotional space if you want: to draw attention to an upcoming performance, a new product launch, or anything else you're proud of and want your friends to know about. (Just be careful not to overdo it—if your status updates start to feel like a steady stream of spam, people may start to tune them out or even defriend you.)

Here are a few very practical ways you can put your status updates to work:

- Access your brain trust by asking questions. My friend Amy, who's just learning Photoshop, used her status to ask for help changing the resolution of a graphic and got responses back in a matter of minutes. I've also seen people request recommendations for doctors, dentists, and other service providers.

- Let people know when you're traveling, so friends in the area you'll be visiting can give a yell if they want to get together with you.

- Remind people about upcoming Events ("Don't forget to reserve your booth for the big craft show, people!")

- Show off a new Web site, video, song, or other content you've just launched.

- Let people know you're all right in the event of something worrisome going on in your corner of the world (earthquake, tornado, campus lockdown) that your friends might hear about.

- Get moral support. Ask for sympathy, positive vibes, or prayers when you're in the hospital, under the weather, or just having a lousy week.

TIP: If you want to include a link in your status update, you can—as long as the URL is short enough to fit the maximum character count. (Facebook will even make it clickable in most of the places your status appears.) For best results, go to TinyURL.com and create a compact version of the URL that won't hog too much room in your status.

Syncing Your Facebook Status with Twitter

If you're a Twitter.com user, you can get double duty out of your Twitter updates by letting them serve as your Facebook status updates, too. Two birds with one tweet!

The easiest way to accomplish this is to install the Twitter application for Facebook. Here's how:

1. Type Twitter in the blue bar's search field.

2. On the results page, find the Twitter application (it should be listed first) and click View Application at the right side of the listing.

Displaying 1 – 10 out of over 500 results for: **twitter**   1 2 3 Next

	Application:	**Twitter**	View Application
	Developer:	Twitter	
	Description:	See what you and your friends are up to on Twitter and update your Twitter status, right from Facebook!	
	Users:	67,081 monthly active users – 19 friends	

3. On the Twitter Application page, click Go to Application.

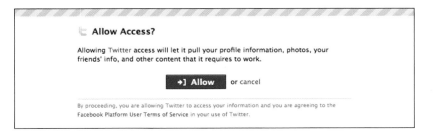

4. In the Allow Access? dialog, click the Allow button to give the Twitter app permission to access your data.

> **NOTE:** Status updates are meant to be timely in nature. So to keep things fresh, if you don't change your status for a full week, Facebook will automatically clear it for you at the seven-day mark.

> **TIP:** You can also update your Facebook status from your mobile phone. (See the *Going Mobile* chapter for more info.)

5. The app will ask you to log in using the user name and password for your Twitter account.

6. Once you've logged in, you'll arrive at the Twitter app's Home page. You can type your update in the field at the top of the page and click the Update button when you're ready.

> **NOTE:** Twitter limits you to 140 characters per update, which is slightly less than the 160 or so that Facebook allows. So if you'd like to post an update in both places, it's best to use the Twitter app, or post it on Twitter first, to make sure it will fit.

7. Once you do that, your update will automatically be posted to both your Facebook status and your Twitter.com account.

> **NOTE:** When your Facebook status update is posted using Twitter, it carries a *via Twitter* tag, as shown at left.

Word of Face: Reaching Your Audience on Facebook

Facebook's News Feeds are a big part of what makes the site so entertaining and addictive. But thanks to a nifty phenomenon called *passive endorsement*, they can also make Facebook a powerful tool for spreading the word about—well, almost anything.

I know, I know. Passive endorsement sounds like a corporate buzz phrase. Something your boss might make you watch a bad training video about. But bear with me—because if you've got a creative project, a business, or a cause to promote on Facebook, passive endorsement can add extra oomph to your efforts.

Here's how it works. Suppose you see an ad for a movie on TV. That's *active endorsement*—the advertisers are deliberately promoting the film to you, with the explicit goal of persuading you to see it. For your part, you know you're being advertised to, so you take whatever claims are made about the movie with a grain of salt. ("One of the year's best, huh? We'll see about *that!*")

On the other hand, suppose you overhear several of your co-workers chatting about seeing the movie—saying how hilarious and moving and thought-provoking it was. Assuming they're people whose opinions you respect, your ears perk up a little and you think, Hmm, maybe I need to check that out.

That's the impact of passive endorsement. Your co-workers didn't collar you and order you to go see the movie—which might have been counterproductive. They simply expressed their sincere appreciation for it.

On Facebook, this effect can manifest itself in a wide variety of ways. If you keep an eye on the News Feed, you'll see stories when friends of yours join a Group, become a fan of a Page, or plan to attend an Event. Third-party apps generate stories, too: If your friends buy tickets for a concert using iLike, add a book to their Visual Bookshelf, or decide to support an organization using Causes, Facebook's News Feed will tell you about it.

How can you make use of this? Here's an example: Suppose you're planning a big benefit for a local organization you're on the board of. You've arranged for superb food and lined up top-notch entertainment. You know your guests will be getting their money's worth; all you have to do is get the word out.

When it's time to promote the event, you can send invitations to the organization's mailing list. You might pass the invite along to your personal friends, too. And you might even ask everyone who gets the invitation to pass it along to all of *their* friends—which would exponentially increase your audience. But will they really do that? Odds are that some of your most loyal friends will pass the invitation along, but most will feel they've done their part just by buying their own tickets.

Now suppose that you post the same event on Facebook and send invites to everyone in your Friends list who might be interested. Each time one of them clicks Yes to accept, Facebook generates a News Feed story saying, "Virgil Brown is attending the 4th Annual Disco Lasagna Bowl Benefit" (subject to their chosen privacy settings, of course). Which allows each person who accepts the invite to passively endorse it, thus helping to spread the word about it to all of *their* Facebook friends. And suddenly your benefit is going viral, reaching a whole new level of exposure.

Obviously, it's possible to substitute all kinds of events in the above scenario: a nightclub party, a poetry slam, a performance by your band, an exhibition of your artwork, or the grand opening of a new business you're launching.

It works the same for any Groups and Pages you may create to promote (for example) a band or a comedy group or a coffeehouse or a freelance photography studio. As you'll see in upcoming chapters, Groups and Pages give you great tools for communicating with fans and customers; but they also allow those fans and customers to announce their loyalty to you via News Feed when they decide to join your Group or become a fan of your Page.

That's a kind of advertising you can't buy—but if your fans and customers love what you do, on Facebook they can choose to give it to you for free.

Admittedly, tapping into the power of passive endorsement can be a little like trying to bottle lightning. It's not enough just to create a Group, a Page, or an Event on Facebook—passive endorsement only works if your content is compelling enough to engage people's interest and strike a collective nerve.

But then again, if you're looking to promote something on Facebook, hopefully you've already done the prerequisite work of analyzing what your audience is interested in and creating something that will appeal to them. In that case, you've got nothing to lose by putting it out there where Facebook users can choose to embrace it—and much to gain if you do manage to tap into a massive wave of passive endorsement.

Notes: Blogging on Facebook

TIP: On the Notes application's Home page, you'll see a roundup of all the Notes recently posted by your friends. So even when you don't have a Note to write yourself, dropping in here can be a good way to catch up on what your friends are writing. You can also click the My Notes link at the top of the page to see all the Notes you've written in the past, and the Notes About Me link to see any Notes in which you've been tagged by your friends.

If you've got a message you'd like to share with your friends that's too long for a status update, Facebook's Notes application has you covered. Writing a Note is Facebook's answer to blogging. You can use Notes to share deep thoughts or goofy non sequiturs, political rants, personal journal entries, poems of the day, or anything else you might post on a blog.

When you post your Note, it will appear on your profile and also in the News Feeds of your friends.

How to Post a Note

There are a couple of different ways to post a Note on Facebook. For the most full-featured Note-writing experience, you can go into the Notes application itself—accessible via the Applications pop-up menu in the Applications bar. (Notes is one of the basic Facebook applications that comes with your account by default, so you don't have to worry about installing it.) To start writing your Note, click the Write a New Note button at the right of the page.

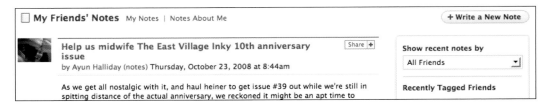

Tag, You're It

What does it mean to tag someone? Anyone whose name you enter in the "Tag people" field will get a Notification telling them that you've tagged them—so it's essentially a way of saying, "Hey, come look at this." You should think of tagging as the Facebook equivalent of tapping someone on the shoulder—which can be annoying if you don't have a good reason for doing it. So it's best to use the tagging feature sparingly and tag people only if they're actually mentioned in the Note or there's some other reason they'd want to know right away that you posted it. If you repeatedly tag people in your Notes for no good reason, they may start ignoring your tags altogether.

On the next page you'll find an easy form with fields for the title and body of the Note. Down at the bottom there's a Photo control that lets you upload a picture from your computer to illustrate the Note. And on the right side is a field that lets you tag any of your friends who are mentioned in the Note.

If you'd like to take your Note beyond the realm of plain text, you can spruce it up with boldface, italics, and other styles using HTML tags. There's a handy cheat sheet that shows you what HTML tags are available, and how they work, which you can access by clicking the small link that says "Feeling bold? Format your note" down at the bottom of the Body field. A privacy control at the bottom of the form lets you specify who can view the Note.

If you're in a hurry, you can also conveniently write a Note right from your Profile page using the Write Note button on the Publisher. The Publisher's simplified Note-writing form gives you two fields, one for the title of the Note and one for the body. Clicking the More Options link adds the controls for tagging, privacy, and uploading a photo.

The Write a Note page in the Notes app gives you all the controls for writing, formatting, tagging, and setting the privacy of your Note.

TIP: If you already have a blog outside of Facebook, you can use your RSS feed to import posts from your blog to Facebook as Notes. See the "Importing Stories to Your Profile from Other Sites" section, later in this chapter.

Posted Items: Sharing Links on Facebook

If you're like me, several times a week (maybe even several times a day) you find yourself reading a fascinating news story, or a witty or insightful blog post, or watching a hilarious video on YouTube, and thinking: "This is brilliant—other people need to see this!"

So how do you share the link with your friends? You could forward it to them via e-mail—but if you do that too often, you run the risk of annoying your friends by cluttering up their already overstuffed inboxes. (And if e-mail has proven anything, it's that one person's brilliant "joke of the day" is another person's spam to be deleted unread.)

Fortunately, Facebook gives you a much less intrusive and more convenient way to share links with your friends: the Posted Items application. (Like the Notes application, Posted Items is one of Facebook's basic apps and is installed to your account from the get-go.) When you post a link using Posted Items, it appears on your profile and also goes out to your friends' News Feeds. So your friends will see it the next time they check their Home page, without feeling like you've spammed them.

Posted Items even get their own dedicated tab in the News Feed area of the Home page, so you and your friends can easily keep track of each other's recommended links for reading and browsing. In a sense, the Posted Items tab is a kind of collaborative group blog that you and your friends create together, each and every day.

How to Post a Link

There are a number of different ways to post links on Facebook, but the most obvious route is to go to the Publisher at the top of your profile and click the Share Link button (which is really an alias for the Posted Items application).

> **TIP:** When you post a YouTube video to Facebook, you don't need the full embed code like you would if you were posting it on your blog or on MySpace. (In fact, if you try to use the embed code it will show up as gibberish when you post it.) All you need is the regular URL for the video. Enter that in the Link field, and Facebook will magically turn it into the embedded video player.

👤 Update Status	🔗 Share Link	🖼 Add Photos	🎥 Add Video	📝 Write Note ▾

http:// | Preview

Enter the URL for the link you'd like to share, and click the Preview button to see how your Posted Item will appear on your Wall and in the News Feed.

remove

Choose a Thumbnail

◀ ▶   2 of 4

THE HEAD OF ORPHEUS: A Russell Hoban Reference Page

A reference for those interested in the works of novelist Russell Hoban, including reviews, commentary, bio, photos, news, and quotations.

http://www.ocelotfactory.com/hoban/...

☐ No Picture

Write an optional comment... | Post

> **TIP:** As you're browsing the Web, you may notice that these days, lots of sites provide their own Share buttons to make it easy for you to post their content to Facebook and other sites like Digg and Delicious. For example, clicking the Share link on any story on the *New York Times* site displays several buttons for sharing the link—including one for Facebook that opens the Posted Items form.

You can edit the text for a Posted Item by clicking in the text area, which will turn it into an editable field. Choose a photo to illustrate the Posted Item by clicking the arrow buttons to cycle through the available choices, or click the No Picture checkbox if none of the photos are appropriate.

You can also type a comment of your own in the box at the bottom of the form. Whatever you type here will appear just below your Posted Item, so you can use this feature to direct your friends' attention to something specific about it, let them know why you wanted to bring it to their notice, or just editorialize a little. When you're happy with how it looks, click the Post button.

Using the Share Button

You don't necessarily have to head back to your Wall to post an item on Facebook. If the link you'd like to post is on Facebook itself—such as a Group, an Event, a Page, a Note, a photo or video, or even someone's profile—you can just look for the handy Share button that Facebook thoughtfully provides on most pages of the site.

You can find the Share button lurking somewhere on most of the pages on Facebook.

When you click the Share button, you'll get a Share dialog with two choices:

NOTE: If you want to post a link on a friend's Wall, you can use the Publisher area of their Profile page to do it—unless your friend has disabled the ability to do this in their Privacy settings.

Only people who are friends with that person will be able to visit your friend's Wall to see what you've posted there. However, a story about the link you've posted may also appear in the News Feeds of your own set of friends, just as if you'd posted the link to your own profile.

- **Send a Message** lets you share the link privately, with one or more specific people, by sending them a direct Inbox message with the Posted Item attached.
- **Post to Profile** shares the item publicly, as a Posted Item—just like using the Publisher.

Using the Share Bookmarklet

If the link you want to post is on a site other than Facebook, there's still a handy way to post it without navigating back to your Wall: the Share Bookmarklet. It's a special button you can add to the Bookmarks toolbar of your Web browser. The Share Bookmarklet works just like the Share button: Wherever you are on the Web, all you have to do is click the bookmarklet and Facebook's Posted Items form will pop up.

To install the Share Bookmarklet, go to the Posted Items application (accessible via the Applications menu) and look for this box.

> **Share on Facebook**
>
> Drag the button above to your Bookmarks Bar to quickly share content with your friends.
>
> More details »

Clicking the "More details" link will display full instructions for whatever browser you're using. (The instructions shown here are for Firefox.)

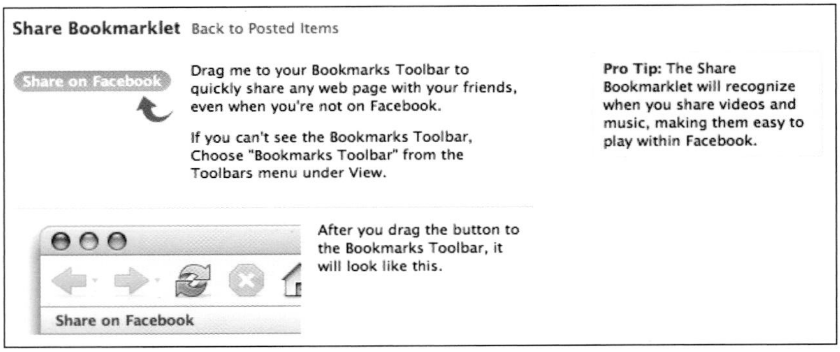

Share Bookmarklet Back to Posted Items

Share on Facebook

Drag me to your Bookmarks Toolbar to quickly share any web page with your friends, even when you're not on Facebook.

If you can't see the Bookmarks Toolbar, Choose "Bookmarks Toolbar" from the Toolbars menu under View.

Pro Tip: The Share Bookmarklet will recognize when you share videos and music, making them easy to play within Facebook.

After you drag the button to the Bookmarks Toolbar, it will look like this.

Share on Facebook

Importing Stories to Your Profile from Other Sites

TIP: If you have trouble importing your blog, consult Facebook's Help center (via the Help link in the footer) for some tips and troubleshooting advice.

You can use the magic of RSS feeds to import activity from a range of popular sites to your Facebook profile—including photos you've posted to Flickr, stories you've recommended on Digg, reviews you've written on Yelp, videos you've posted on YouTube, posts from your outside blog—and automatically turn this content into stories posted to your profile.

To see the available options, go to the Publisher and click the Import button.

NOTE: Whether Facebook imports some or all of your previous activity on an external site or blog depends on what it's able to access from the feed.

Wall   Info   Photos   **+**

👤 Update Status   🔁 Share Link   🖼 Add Photos   🎥 Add Video   📡 Import   ▼

Available Sites:

●● Flickr   Digg   Picasa   Delicious   Yelp   Google Reader

YouTube   StumbleUpon   Last.fm   P Pandora   h hulu   Blog/RSS

Then click the button for the site you'd like to import content from. If you're choosing to import activity from a site like Flickr, Yelp, or YouTube, you'll be asked to enter the user name associated with your account for that site. Facebook will then import some or all of your previous activity on the site, depending on what the feed makes available to it.

●● Enter the user name associated with your **Flickr** account.

User Name: [   ]   **Import**   or Cancel

If you'd like to import an existing blog, you'll be asked to enter its public URL. Facebook will import your previous blog posts as individual Notes.

📶 Enter the public URL associated with your **Blog/RSS** account. Please only import your own blog.

Public URL: [|]   **Import**   or Cancel

Once you enable importing, Facebook will continue to import activity every time you update the account or blog that you've enabled. If you want to stop importing at any point in the future, you can disable it by reversing the operation: Click the Import button on the Publisher, and then click the button for the site you want to stop importing from.

Commenting on Facebook Stories

Facebook's feed stories aren't just one-way telegrams transmitted to your friends—they can also be conversation starters. Certain kinds of feed stories, including status updates and Posted Items, have Comment links that appear underneath each story when it shows up on someone's Wall or in the News Feed on the Home page.

Eli Bishop is watching the dog try to play with three toys at once.
12 hours ago – Comment

Clicking the Comment link allows people to type a short response to the story, creating a discussion thread about it.

((•)) **WARNING:** If you post a comment and then have second thoughts about it, you can delete it from Facebook by clicking the little X at the upper-right side of your comment. But remember that Facebook's default setting is to send you an e-mail notification whenever someone comments on a story about you. So the friend whose story you've just commented on may very well see your comment in e-mail form *regardless of whether you delete it or not.* Moral: Think before you click!

TIP: In addition to deleting comments you make on other people's stories, you're allowed to delete any comments your friends make on stories about you.

Your Place or Mine?

When someone writes on your Wall, should you answer them on your own Wall or theirs? This is a question that frequently puzzles Facebook newcomers, and occasionally provokes etiquette debates among old-timers, too.

These days at least, the answer depends on whether it's a regular Wall post or a comment on something you've posted.

Before Facebook introduced comments, the prevailing etiquette was that if someone wrote on your Wall, you answered them on their own Wall in order to make sure they'd see the answer. And that's still a good rule of thumb for Wall posts that aren't comments attached to a specific story. (See "Can You Write on Your Own Wall?" earlier in this chapter, for more on this.)

But when someone comments on a story on your Wall, the ideal place to answer them is in the same comment thread. This keeps the discussion organized in one central place, which makes it easier to follow for everyone. And because Facebook automatically notifies you when someone replies to a thread you've already commented on, you don't have to worry that your friend won't see your answer—they'll get a tap on the shoulder from Facebook.

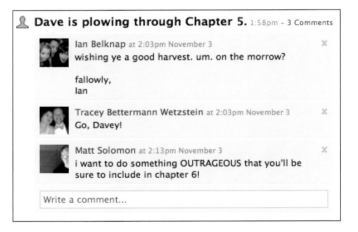

When you click the Status Updates tab on the Home page, you'll be able to see the discussion threads that have sprung up about your friends' statuses, in addition to the statuses themselves. The same is true for the Posted Items tab, as well as many of the items that show up in the News Feed and Live Feed tabs. (Photos have comments as well, but to see them you'll need to click on the photo in question to go to its page.) And of course, each comment thread is visible on the Wall of the person the story is about.

These comment threads are where you'll find some of the liveliest and most entertaining interaction on Facebook. If you're bored and looking for some banter with a friend, starting or joining in on a comment thread is always a good bet.

By default, Facebook sends you a notification each time someone comments on a story about you or something you've posted. And if you comment on a story about one of your friends, Facebook will notify you of all subsequent comments on that thread—making it easy to keep following the discussion and any responses that your own comment may have provoked.

6

Communicating on Facebook

Public conversations—the ones that take place on Walls or in comment threads—are where most of the really fun interaction happens on Facebook. But there are also times when it's necessary to take the conversation somewhere private—either because you need to have a one-on-one conversation with someone, or because you want to communicate with a small group of friends without the whole world listening in.

So in this chapter, we'll look at the tools Facebook gives you for private communication, including Inbox messages and Facebook's Chat application.

But wait, there's more! Communicating on Facebook doesn't just happen in words—it happens in pictures, too, which are called Gifts, and special nonverbal messages called Pokes. So we'll take a look at some of the ways Facebook lets you substitute a Poke or a picture for a thousand words (give or take).

And to round things out, we'll talk a little about the dynamics and etiquette of interpersonal communication on Facebook.

Direct Messages: The Ins and Outs of the Facebook Inbox

WARNING: When you check your Facebook Inbox, be on your guard for suspicious messages, and be careful about clicking on links contained in Facebook messages. You may receive messages that appear to come from one of your friends but are actually sent by phishers who've gained access to your friend's account. Some Facebook messages may also be generated by viruses, and contain links to Trojan horses or other malware. See the *Privacy and Security* chapter for more details and some tips on how to spot suspicious messages.

You can think of your Facebook Inbox as being like an e-mail account that's built right into Facebook. Just like regular e-mail, Facebook's Inbox lets you send and receive direct electronic messages addressed to specific people.

But there are a couple of important differences. For one thing, Facebook messages allow you to contact someone without knowing their e-mail address. You can send messages to anyone on Facebook that you're friends with, or anyone for whom you can see a Send a Message link in search results. This feature allows you to contact someone without necessarily revealing your own e-mail address, which may be useful if you don't know the person well.

Facebook messages also make it easy to attach items, such as links, videos, or Gifts (defined and discussed later in this chapter), using the Facebook interface to generate handy embedded previews.

| facebook | Home | Profile | Friends | Inbox 6 | | Dave Awl | Settings | Logout |

| **Inbox** | Sent Messages | Notifications | Updates | | | **+ Compose Message** |

Select: --- ▾   Mark as Unread   Mark as Read   Delete   🔍 Search Inbox

● ☐ **Ian Belknap**
Yesterday at 1:03pm   🖼 re: Illustrator?
Hey, Creativos – The company I work for, The Neo–Futurist...   x

● ☐ **Matt Solomon**
Sun 10:38am   **re: THESE ARE THE SQUIDS I WARNED YOU ABOUT!!!**
they said they'd just be here for the weekend, but they w...   x

↩ ☐ **Kevin Spengel**
November 14 at 3:04am   📷 re: Comments on my new blog
Would y'all give me some honest feedback to improve on my...   x

↩ ☐ **Suzie Nasol**
November 12 at 4:09pm   re: status check
OK. Thanks for the update!   x

☐ **Myopic Books Poetry Reading
Series, Chicago**
November 12 at 6:21am   This Sunday @ Myopic Books, Brandi Homan & Katy Lederer
MYOPIC POETRY SERIES, a weekly series of readings and occ...   x

How to Check Your Messages

When you've got Facebook mail, you'll see a number appear next to the word *Inbox* in the blue bar, telling you how many unread messages are waiting.

Click Inbox to go to your Inbox and view your messages. Once there, you can click on the subject line of any message to read it. (You can also click on the name of the sender to take a look at their profile.)

Message Indicators

Facebook gives you some handy indicators to let you see the status of each message in your Inbox at a glance. (See the screen shot on the facing page for examples of these.)

- A blue dot next to a message means it's a new, unread message. (Unread messages will also be shaded in blue.)
- A curvy arrow next to a message means it's a message you've already replied to. (In the case of a group message, it means you were the last person in the conversation to reply.)
- If the message includes an attachment, an icon next to the subject line will tell you what kind of attachment. A photo icon indicates that there's an image attached, a bookmark icon indicates that there's a link attached, and so forth.

Managing Messages

Next to each message thread in your Inbox is a checkbox that you can use to change its status from Read to Unread (or vice versa), or delete the message.

Dig Those Crazy Threads
Facebook messages are organized into threads—much like the discussion threads on News Feed and Wall stories. Each line in your Inbox represents one thread, which contains an original message as well as all of the replies to that message. So if you send your friend Matt a message, and the two of you get into a conversation that runs to 20 replies—possibly spread out over several days—all that back-and-forth won't take up 21 lines scattered all through your Inbox. Instead, there'll be one line for the entire thread, and when you click on it, all 21 messages will be there, in chronological order. This helps keep your Inbox organized and means you don't have to wade through so much clutter to find what you're looking for.

NOTE: Although you can delete a thread from your Inbox, this action may not always be permanent. If another participant in the thread sends a new reply, the thread will appear in your Inbox again.

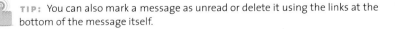

Simply select the checkboxes for one or more messages, and then click the appropriate action at the top of the page. The Select pop-up menu lets you select certain types of messages so that you can mark or delete them en masse. This is handy if you want to delete all of the messages you've already read, for example, or mark all of your unread messages as read in order to reset the number of new messages displayed in the blue bar.

TIP: You can also mark a message as unread or delete it using the links at the bottom of the message itself.

TIP: Marking a message as unread after you've read it can come in handy when you don't have time to respond right at the moment. That way it'll remain in the count of unread messages displayed in the blue bar, taunting you until you do come back and answer it.

The Sorting Hat
At the time of this writing, Facebook doesn't give you a lot of tools for organizing or archiving your messages. There's no way, for example, to file your messages away into customized mailboxes or folders. You also can't flag them (other than marking them as unread), assign them levels of priority, or easily forward them. So if you're the sort of person who likes to keep a well-organized, backed-up archive of all your correspondence, you might prefer to use conventional e-mail for important messages where you do know the e-mail addresses of the other participants.

Who Can You Message?
In the To field of the Compose New Message form, you can type the name of a friend (which Facebook will attempt to recognize and autocomplete for you) or a Friend List (as long as it has fewer than 20 friends on it).

If you'd like to include a friend who isn't on Facebook in your message, you can do that, too—just go ahead and enter their e-mail address in the To field, and they'll receive your message as e-mail.

If you want to send a message to someone on Facebook whom you haven't already friended, and whose e-mail address you don't know, you can do it only by clicking the Send a Message link on their profile, or in search results.

Tabs: Sent Messages, Notifications, Updates

In addition to the default view of the Inbox, which shows you messages you've received from others, there are three other views you can access by clicking the tabs across the top of the Inbox.

- **The Sent Messages tab** shows you the messages you've sent to others.
- **The Notifications tab** gives you quick access to your Notifications page, where you can see the recent notifications you've received from Facebook as well as those from third-party apps (as mentioned way back in the *Anatomy of Facebook* chapter).
- **The Updates tab** shows you all of the update messages you've received from any Facebook Pages you've chosen to become a fan or supporter of. (See the *Pages and Ads* chapter for full info on updates—how they work and how to send them from Pages you create.)

Searching the Inbox

Facebook gives you a field at the top of your Inbox (for both the Inbox and Sent Messages tabs) that lets you search through your messages to zero in on what you're looking for. You can search by name (to find all the messages to or from a certain person) as well as by keyword (to find all of the messages related to summer band camp, or a Facebook Group you're a member of, or mollusks, for example).

How to Compose and Send an Inbox Message

If you're already in the Inbox, click the Compose Message button at the right side of the page. From any other page on Facebook, the quickest method is to hover your pointer over the Inbox link in the blue bar until the pop-up menu appears, and then choose Compose New Message.

 TIP: You can also send someone a message using the Send *Name* a Message link on their Profile page, which usually appears right below their profile picture.

Inbox	Sent Messages	Notifications	Updates		Compose Message

To:

Subject:

Message:

Attach: 📹 Record Video   📺 Share Link   ✴ Add Flowers

🖼 Add Have a panda!   ✉ Add British Gifts   ✏ Add Poetry Stuff

🦋 Add Beautiful Butt...   ▾ more

[Send]   [Cancel]

Once you arrive at the Compose Message form, all you have to do is fill in the To, Subject, and Message fields. You can also choose to add an attachment using the buttons at the bottom of the form.

The Record Video link lets you add a short video clip to your message, using a camera attached to your computer.

The Share Link button lets you attach a Web link, much like using the Posted Items application (as described in the *Wall, Status, and News Feeds* chapter). Enter the URL in the Link field, and click Attach; Facebook will generate a preview to show you how the attachment will look at the bottom of the message. You can use the arrow buttons to cycle through the available images from the page you're linking to, and you can click the accompanying text to edit it. If you decide you want to get rid of the attachment altogether, you can click the Remove link to delete it.

You may also see buttons for some of your authorized apps, which allow you to attach gift images, music videos, or other goodies to your message.

NOTE: Anything you attach to an Inbox message is private, just like the message itself, and won't show up as a story on your Wall or in your News Feed.

WARNING: You are allowed to send Inbox messages to people whom you aren't friends with. But be careful not to abuse this privilege. If you send too many messages to people you don't know, or Facebook receives complaints that you're sending unwanted messages to strangers, Facebook may take away your messaging privileges or even deactivate your account. Also note that when you send someone you're not friends with an Inbox message, that person is temporarily granted access to your Facebook profile, so they can check you out and see who they're talking to.

TIP: You can't add someone to a group message thread once it's already in progress. So if you're talking to your friends Tracey and Stacey and you suddenly realize that your other friend Amy would totally love this conversation, you'll need to start a new group message that includes her—and then catch her up on what's been said so far.

Group Messages and Branched Threads: Who Do You Think You're Talking To?

You can address messages to more than one friend at a time—up to 20 friends per message—which is convenient if there's something you want to share with a select group of friends.

When you answer a group message, it's *verrry* important to be aware of whether you're talking to one person in the thread, or the whole group. Anecdotes abound about Facebookers who thought they were talking one-on-one, and then discovered that their flirty or gossipy messages were being read by the entire group instead of the one person they thought they had replied to.

By default, if you simply type your reply in the box at the bottom of the message thread and then click the Send button, you'll be sending your reply to everyone in the group. (Hence the sneaky Reply All label directly above the response field.)

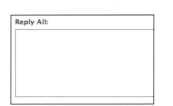

The reply box for a group message is labeled Reply All to let you know your response will be seen by everyone the original message was addressed to.

If you want to reply directly to one person, you need to create a *branched thread.* You can do that by clicking the Reply link underneath the person's name, next to one of their contributions to the thread. A new message form will open up for the branched thread, which is now strictly between you and the person whose Reply link you clicked.

You can tell when you're reading a branched thread because at the top of the screen you'll see the notice shown below. Clicking the "Show thread history" link will let you see the group message the new thread was split off from.

Clicking the Reply link next to the name of the sender (or any other participant in the thread) will create a branched thread, so that your message is seen only by that person.

This message is branched from a previous thread. Show thread history.

Chatting on Facebook

Facebook provides its own built-in Chat application, so you can have real-time conversations with your Facebook friends. If you've ever chatted online using an application such as AOL Instant Messenger, MSN Messenger, Yahoo Messenger, or iChat, then the mechanics of Facebook Chat will be very familiar to you. But even if you're new to Chat, it's not too tough to figure out.

Going Online (and Seeing Who Else Is Online)

The first step to chatting with a friend on Facebook is to change your own Chat availability to Online. You can do that by clicking the Chat icon at the right side of the Application bar at the bottom of your screen. When the Chat

The icon for Facebook Chat lives just to the right of the Notifications icon, at the right side of the Applications bar. Click the Chat icon for a pop-up menu that will allow you to change your Chat availability and set other options.

menu pops up, click the link that says Go Online. You'll see the indicator dot change from red to green, indicating that you're online and available for chat; and an Online Friends pop-up menu will appear in the Applications bar —telling you at a glance how many of your friends are currently online.

When you click the Online Friends menu, you'll see a listing that shows you which of your friends are available for chat. A green dot next to a friend means they're online and have been recently active on Facebook. A half-moon means your friend is idle—which means that they haven't taken any action on Facebook within the last 10 minutes. (Which in turn is a clue that even though they've set their status to online, they might have stepped away from their computer.)

How to Start a Chat

Starting a chat is easy. Just choose the friend you'd like to chat with in the Online Friends menu and click their name to open a new chat window.

Starting a new chat: Type your first message in the field at the bottom of the Chat window, press the Return/Enter key, and wait for a response. Once your friend answers, you can continue to enter your own responses in the same field until the two of you run out of delightfully witty things to say.

How to Minimize or Close a Chat Window

Clicking the Hide Chat Window icon at the top of the window (it looks like a dash) will collapse the window down to a minimized icon in your Application bar. You can click on the mimimized chat icon to reopen it at any time. While the chat window is minimized, a balloon icon will appear to let you know of any new responses the person you're chatting with enters. The balloon displays a number that tells you exactly how many responses are waiting.

Click Go Online in the Chat pop-up menu to make yourself available.

The Online Friends pop-up menu shows you who's available to chat. Notice that Kevin's name shows a half-moon instead of a green dot, because he hasn't been active on Facebook in the last 10 minutes.

A minimized Chat window appears just to the left of the Online Friends menu in the Applications bar. You can click the minimized window to restore it to full size at any time.

A number balloon lets you know how many new responses are waiting in the minimized Chat window.

TIP: Facebook doesn't allow you to chat with anyone who isn't in your Friends list. The only ways you can directly contact non-friends on Facebook are through Inbox messages or friend requests.

How to Pop Out a Chat Window

If you'd like a larger Chat window (which allows you to see more of the conversation without scrolling), just click the Pop Out Chat link in the main Chat menu. Presto, a full-size chat window will open up. You can return it to the small size by clicking the Pop In link.

NOTE: Facebook's Chat application is built for simplicity, so at present it's not as full-featured as the free-standing chat applications you may be used to. For one thing, there's no way to block specific friends from seeing that you're online (other than to defriend them altogether) or allow only a select group to know that you're online. You're either available to everyone in your Friends list, or to no one. Also, Facebook Chat allows you to chat with only one friend in any given conversation (although you can have multiple chat conversations active at the same time). Facebook says on its Help page that some of this missing functionality may be added in the future.

How to View and Clear Your Chat History

When you start a new conversation with a friend you've chatted with before, you'll be able to see the last few lines of your most recent conversation in the chat window. (Currently there's no way to view or access older conversations.) If you want a blank slate, you can delete that history by clicking the Clear Chat History link at the top of the window.

Other Chat Settings

Clicking the Settings link (at the top of the Chat icon's pop-up menu) displays a few additional options you may find useful:

- **Show Feed Stories in Chat** allows stories about you or the friend you're chatting with to appear in the Chat window. (This may provide fodder for your conversation.)

- **Play Sound for New Messages** allows Facebook to get your attention with an alert sound when someone sends you a new message via chat.
- **Keep Online Friends Window Open** changes the behavior of the Online Friends window. With this box deselected, the window automatically closes when you click elsewhere on the page. If this box is selected, the window stays open until you choose to minimize it by clicking the dash icon in the upper-right corner. (This checkbox is visible only when your chat availability is set to Online.)
- **Show Only Names in Online Friends** hides the profile pictures in the Online Friends window, which saves space and allows you to see more of the list without scrolling.

Click the Settings link at the top of the Chat icon's pop-up menu to reveal these checkboxes.

Poking and Getting Poked

Facebook has added its own distinctive entry to the lexicon of nonverbal communication: the Poke. Sending someone a Poke on Facebook is just a simple greeting—a way of saying hello without really having anything else in particular to say. You might poke someone when you want to get their attention, let them know you're thinking about them, or simply remind them that you exist. It can serve as a hug, a tickle, a tap on the shoulder, or an impatient tap of the foot.

When you get poked by someone, the Poke shows up in the right-hand column on your Home page.

> **Pokes**
> You were poked by:
> Becca Freed – poke back | remove

You then have the option to poke the person back or simply remove the Poke. You can also leave it there for as long as you want, until you decide how you want to respond. (Sometimes I leave a Poke on my Home page as a handy quick link to the profile of someone I owe some attention to—a string-around-the-finger reminder.)

How to Send a Poke

When you find yourself in a poking mood, just navigate to the profile of the person you'd like to poke, and find the Poke *Name* link (usually right under their profile picture). Click the link, and then click Poke in the confirmation dialog that opens. Once you do that, your friend is as good as poked.

Caveat Poker
The ambiguity of the basic Facebook Poke makes it something of a Rorschach test. It's possible that the person you send your Poke to will read something different into it from what you intended, especially if you don't know them very well. They might think you're flirting when you just meant to say hello, or telling them to hurry up with their next Scrabble move when you actually meant to flirt. So you might want to take that into consideration before you poke, and if you want to make sure your message isn't misunderstood, use a more explicit form of communication.

Advanced Pokeology

TIP: Once upon a time, you were allowed to poke anybody you could find by searching on Facebook. But in recent times Facebook has reined in the Poke feature. These days, you can poke only those people whose profiles you're allowed to access.

The basic Facebook Poke, as iconic as it is, doesn't get as much play as it used to, because a number of third-party apps have sprung up to let you poke people in more specific and less ambiguous ways. The most popular and enduring of these is probably the SuperPoke application, which lets you choose from a wide variety of things you'd like to do to your friends—from nice to silly to mock-aggressive—and then send your friend a short message telling them what you've just (virtually) done unto them. Your friend then has the option to do something back unto you.

TIP: As with any app you're interested in, you can find and install SuperPoke by typing its name in the search field in the blue bar.

Just a few examples of the many things you can do to your friends using SuperPoke

An example of a Wall story announcing a SuperPoke

What Are You, a Mind Reader?

Speaking of nonverbal communications and ambiguous messages, here's a rule of thumb you may find useful: You'll have a better time on Facebook if you don't spend too much time reading between the lines, or reading things into the actions your friends do or don't take on Facebook.

Sure, it's easy to be paranoid and jump to the conclusion that someone ignored your Poke or your friend request because they dislike you. Or that a friend failed to RSVP to your Event invitation because they're trying to avoid spending time with you. Or that another friend didn't respond to the song you dedicated to them using the iLike music app because they secretly loathe your taste in music.

But it's just as possible that your friend is merely having trouble keeping up with all the invitations and Pokes

they're receiving these days. Maybe they had a bad day, aren't feeling well, or are traveling at the moment and don't have reliable Internet access. Maybe they're having difficulty figuring out the semiotics of Facebook. Or maybe they just accidentally clicked the wrong button.

The point is, unless someone tells you point-blank that you're on their D-list or you've ticked them off, you can't reliably deduce that from their Facebook behavior. Assuming the worst will only get you ulcers, and maybe wind up doing real damage to a friendship that is perfectly healthy.

So cut your friends plenty of slack. And spend your Facebook time focusing on the Facebook friends who *do* return your Pokes.

Facebook Gifts: When a Picture Is Worth a Hundred Cents

When you'd like to let someone on Facebook know you're thinking about them—either because it's their birthday or some other special occasion, or just because you want to brighten their day—you can send them a Gift.

Gifts, in Facebook's lexicon, are small images that you can select (from a wide array of possibilities) and send to a friend along with an optional message of greeting. (See the sidebar "Why Send Someone a Picture of a Cupcake?" for more on the nature and purpose of Gifts.)

TIP: The free Gifts in Facebook's Gift application are generally sponsored by Facebook's advertisers for promotional purposes—as tie-ins to a movie's advertising campaign, for example. The freebies tend to change regularly, so keep an eye on the Gifts app to catch the latest bargains.

Viewing and Managing Gifts

When you receive a Gift, where and how it appears depends on whether the Gift has been designated by the sender as Private, Public, or Anonymous.

- **Public Gifts** are displayed in the recipient's Gifts box, which appears on their profile (unless they've chosen to remove it). The Gift also shows up as a story on the recipient's Wall. Public Gifts are visible to anyone who's allowed to view the recipient's profile, according to their privacy settings.

- **Private Gifts** also appear in the Gifts box, but the name of the sender and any message they've included are hidden from everyone but the recipient. Only the image itself is visible to others. No Wall story is generated for a Private Gift.

- **Anonymous Gifts** show up in the Gifts box, but no Wall story appears. If there's a message, it's visible only to the recipient. And because the Gift is anonymous, the sender's name is hidden from even the recipient.

You can click any Gift in your Gifts box to read its message (if there is one).

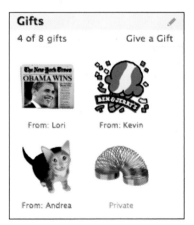

Gifts you receive appear in the Gifts box on your profile. You can click any Gift to read its message, if there is one, and edit or delete it.

If you receive a Gift you don't want displayed in your Gift box, you can delete it (or set its status to Private, if you just want to hide its message) by clicking the Gift itself. You can also view and edit all of your Gifts by clicking the number of Gifts at the top of the Gifts box, or by clicking the My Gifts link within the Gifts app itself.

You can choose to remove the Gifts box from your profile by clicking its Pencil icon. And of course, you can delete any Gift story from your Wall by clicking the little X at the right side of the story.

How to Send a Gift

When the Gift-giving mood strikes you, start by going into the Gifts application. (Gifts is one of the basic Facebook applications that comes pre-installed in your Facebook account by default, so you don't have to add it unless you've previously removed it for some reason.) You can access the Gifts application by clicking its icon in the Application bar's pop-up menu, or by typing *Gifts* in the search box in the blue bar.

Although a few of the Facebook Gifts you can choose to send are free, the vast majority of them have to be purchased using Gift credits—which you can buy from Facebook using your credit card. $1 in U.S. currency buys you 100 Gift credits, and most Facebook Gifts cost 100 credits—so in most cases you'll be spending a buck for each Gift.

Why Send Someone a Picture of a Cupcake?

Newcomers to Facebook are occasionally thrown by the concept of sending someone a picture of something as a gift, at least until they get used to the idea.

Take my friend Susan, who one day, shortly after joining Facebook, changed her status to read, "Susan doesn't really understand the sending of cupcakes on Facebook and won't be participating until it make sense to her." Susan's friends had been greeting her using a popular app called Send Cupcakes, which lets you create a customized cupcake (pick one of several cupcakes, choose a frosting, add a topping)—and then send an image of the final cupcake to a friend.

To Susan, it made no sense whatsoever to send someone a picture of a cupcake they couldn't actually *eat*.

If you share Susan's bewilderment, it may help to think of Facebook's gifts not so much as gifts, but as greeting cards. After all, if you send a friend a card with a picture of a funny kitten on it, you're not sending them an actual kitten—you're sending them the *idea* of a kitten, just to say hello and give them a little lift.

Ultimately, this is all just a variation of what the transactional analysis gurus call *warm fuzzies*. Friends and loved ones are generally looking for ways to send and reinforce the message that they care about each other. If they can entertain each other or make the other person laugh in the process of sending a warm fuzzy, that adds value to the message.

One of the best things about Facebook is that it gives you innumerable interesting ways to send warm fuzzies to the people you care about—and the sending of gifts is a big part of that.

So, if you know that your friend Amy is a big coffee fanatic and you use an app called Send Coffee to send her a grande cappuccino, in addition to letting her know you're thinking about her, you've demonstrated that you know what she likes—a sign of true friendship.

And by the same token, if your brother is a huge fan of the Muppets and you use the Send Muppets app to send him, say, Beaker, then in addition to telling him you love him, you've also sent him the vitally important message *"Meep meep meep meep meep meep."*

CHOOSING A GIFT

Once you're in the Gifts app itself, you'll see a directory of Gifts to choose from in the top part of the page. You can browse various categories of Gifts, including types of Gifts (such as animals, flowers, or sports-related images); Gifts related to birthdays or upcoming holidays; or Gifts appropriate to specific relationships (such as romantic gifts or friendship-themed gifts).

TIP: You can also give someone a Gift using the Publisher. Go to the Wall of the person you'd like to bestow your Gift on, click the Give Gift button on the Publisher, and follow the steps of the Gift-giving process from there.

Underneath each Gift is its price in Gift credits, and if it's a limited edition (meaning it can only be given a certain number of times before it disappears forever from the directory), you'll see the number of copies remaining before it's sold out.

When you've decided on a Gift, click the image to select it. You'll see the name and description of the Gift appear next to the "Add your message" field a bit lower down on the page.

CHOOSING A RECIPIENT

In the "Choose your recipient" field, type the name of the friend you'd like to give the Gift to. Once Facebook identifies the friend whose name you're typing, their Profile picture will appear next to the field.

Choose your recipient:

Lori Dana

Lori Dana
Chicago, IL

ADDING A MESSAGE AND SPECIFYING PRIVACY

If you'd like to include a message with your Gift, type it in the "Add your message" field.

Next, decide whether you want the Gift to be Public, Private, or Anonymous (as explained earlier in the "Viewing and Managing Gifts" section), and click the corresponding button at the bottom of the screen. Then click the Continue button to go on to the next page.

BUYING CREDITS

If you haven't already bought enough credits to pay for the Gift, you'll see a dialog telling you how many credits you need.

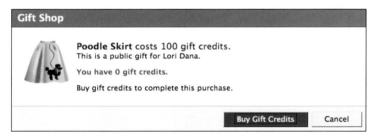

Click the Buy Gift Credits button, and on the next page you'll see a form where you can enter your credit card info and complete the purchase. Once your card info is verified, you'll see a dialog confirming that your Gift has been sent and letting you know how many credits you have left over.

Meanwhile, your Gift will appear in the recipient's Gift box, and a story will appear on their Wall as well as your own (subject to privacy settings).

Cupcakes and Karma: Third-Party Gift Applications

In addition to the Gifts you can send using Facebook's official Gifts app, there are a slew of third-party gift-sending apps you can install that will allow you to send virtual presents to your friends. Even better, these third-party apps generally let you send gifts free of charge, because the developers are looking for exposure and advertising revenue rather than expecting you to cough up your credit card.

The range and diversity of gift apps currently available is downright inspiring. Send Good Karma lets you exchange New Agey icons representing peace, tranquility, enlightenment, or compassion, while Send Sushi lets you offer someone a bowl of miso soup or a dish of maki rolls. Punk Rock Singles lets you send a friend a record by the Clash, the Undertones, or the Buzzcocks, while Beautiful Butterflies lets you present a friend with a Gulf Fritillary or a Many Banded Dagger-Wing. You can give one of your pals Tom Baker's scarf using Doctor Who Gifts, an R2D2 using Star Wars Gifts, or a Lumberjack using Monty Python Gifts.

You can find these apps easily by searching, but in most cases you won't have to, because they spread through Facebook's social continuum virally. Once you've built up your Friends list a little, you'll start receiving requests to accept everything from chocolate cake to Ewoks as gifts, and once you accept them, you'll be able to start sending them out yourself using the app you've just authorized.

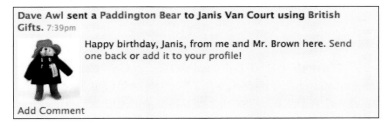

Dave Awl sent a Paddington Bear to Janis Van Court using British Gifts. 7:39pm

Happy birthday, Janis, from me and Mr. Brown here. Send one back or add it to your profile!

Add Comment

An example of a birthday gift I gave to a friend using the British Gifts application

Enlightenment

The Send Good Karma app lets you send your friends abstract blessings such as Peace, Compassion, Happiness, and Enlightenment.

A customized binge trigger created with the Send Cupcakes app. Chocolate with peanut butter icing and bananas on top, yum.

The Retro Gifts app lets you send dyn-o-mite gifts and toys like Lincoln Logs, Tiger Beat *magazine, or the hipster timepiece shown above.*

The Gulf Fritillary from the Beautiful Butterflies application

TIP: See the *Applications and Other Add-Ons* chapter for more info on how to use and manage third-party applications.

The Fine Art of Not Being Obnoxious

Let's get one thing clear: Facebook etiquette can be murky territory. After all, people of diverse ages, backgrounds, levels of computer proficiency, political leanings, and religious perspectives use Facebook, in countries around the world. So there are bound to be some colliding expectations and assumptions about what constitutes polite interaction. But it seems reasonable to start with the assumption that you join Facebook to have fun with your friends, not to annoy them. So here are a few basic tips for playing well with others:

1. **Know your friends.**

The golden rule says that you should do unto others as you would have them do unto you. But here's the rub: On Facebook, not everyone wants to be done unto the same way. You can't assume that just because you enjoy being sent pictures of cupcakes, Muppets, and funny kittens every day of the week, all of your friends do, too. On Facebook, different folks enjoy different kinds of pokes. Some people like word games. Some people like adversarial games that involve pretending to turn each other into vampires, kickboxing, or recruiting each other into the mob. Others prefer gentler, more cooperative pursuits like sending each other plants, or dedicating songs and videos to each other. So it's worth taking a little time to consider your audience before you fire off an invitation or a request. Think before you click.

2. **Know how to take a hint.**

On a related note, sometimes silence speaks louder than words, so it's important to pay attention to the responses you *don't* get from your friends, as well as the ones you do. If you keep inviting a friend to play games with you or install a particular app, and you get no response, take the hint and stop badgering them.

If the responses are slower than you expect, take that into account, too. Some people are naturally more active on Facebook than others. Some people have more time in their day for playing games and socializing, whereas others have to wedge it into a half-hour they've stolen between the time the kids fall asleep and hitting their own wall of exhaustion.

If you pay just a little bit of attention, you'll soon get a sense of which friends want to exchange plants with you on Green Patch several times a week, which pals are always quick to reply to a Wall post, and who generally needs a few days in order to check in and respond. Once you have a good idea of how much time and attention your individual friends can spare, you can tailor your level of interaction to theirs.

Of course, a corollary is that the closer you are to someone, the more you may be able to get away with stretching those boundaries. If it's an old friend you've been through thick and thin with, you may be able to deliberately annoy them with impunity—and they may even find it funny. But that's strictly a swim-at-your-own risk scenario.

3. Treat new friends with extra restraint.

If someone who doesn't know you very well accepts your friend request, they're engaging in an act of trust—taking a chance on you. Don't make them regret their decision by abusing that trust.

That means treating them with kid gloves until you get to know them. When you make a new friend, don't immediately start bombarding them with SuperPokes, app requests, and invitations to Events that require an RSVP. Take things slow. Wait until you have a sense of their likes and dislikes before you start nudging them on a regular basis.

Here's a good rule of thumb: Don't send a new friend a second invitation or request before they've replied to the first one. If you strive for a harmonious 1:1 ratio of requests to responses, you'll most likely avoid ticking your new friend off.

4. Be sensitive to your friends' feelings.

Some people are very private, while others are downright exhibitionists. You may be completely comfortable posting pictures of yourself cavorting on the beach in your Borat thong, or dancing on a table with a bleary grin and a plastic cup in your hand—but some of your friends may be shyer about such things, or have uptight in-laws and bosses to worry about. They may be trusting you to understand that what happened in Vegas was supposed to stay there, rather than happening all over again on Facebook the next day.

Wall posts work the same way. Your friend may love your ribald repartee when you're hanging out one-on-one, but may not be so thrilled to have it posted on their Wall where co-workers, parents, or teenage kids can see it.

So—if you're not sure whether your friend will be comfortable with a photo you'd like to post, take the initiative and ask them about it ahead of time. And if a friend asks you to take a photo down, or they remove their name from its tags, you should respect that unless you have a very good reason not to.

Before you write on someone's Wall, take a moment to remember that it's not a private one-to-one text message—it's more like sticking a note on their front door that the whole neighborhood can see. And if your friend deletes something you wrote on their Wall, cut them some slack. They may very well have laughed out loud, right before they clicked the Delete button.

5. Facebook is not LinkedIn—dress down for success.

It's fine to use Facebook for business purposes—but remember that Facebook is first and foremost a *social* space. Here's what I mean: Suppose you get an invitation to a Hawaiian-themed party. And suppose that you show up to a room full of people in floral shirts and leis dressed in a navy blue business suit, and while the other attendees are learning hula moves and drinking fruity cocktails, you circulate among them thrusting your business card under their noses and attempting to sell them life insurance.

It's fairly likely that after ten or fifteen minutes of that, you'll find yourself propping up a wall by your lonesome, while the other guests scramble to put as much furniture as possible between themselves and you.

That's not to say you can't sell insurance and find willing customers at a party. But you need to use a subtler approach, turn on the charm, and enter into the spirit of the shindig. Once you've chatted with someone for a while, made them laugh a little and gained their trust, you can casually mention what you do for a living and gauge their level of interest without so much risk of being stabbed through the heart with a pineapple-topped toothpick.

The above may not sound like social-skills rocket science, but it's amazing how many people show up to Facebook dressed in their navy blue suit and brandishing their business card—metaphorically speaking.

So do a little reality check. If the Info tab of your profile consists mostly of phrases like "my new teleseminar," "entrepreneurial market niche positioning," and "make money!!!" you might want to humanize it a little by also listing some of your favorite TV shows and bands and things, so you seem a little less like a profit-driven zombie.

Just sayin'.

7

Applications and Other Add-Ons

As a public transportation rider, I don't resort to car metaphors very often. But in this case, it fits: If Facebook is a car, then applications are the options. You can get where you're going using the tools that come with Facebook by default, but adding applications may make the ride more fun, and possibly even more productive.

Some Facebook apps are practical, like the GPS navigator in your dashboard; some add entertainment to the ride, like a built-in stereo; and some are just lighthearted decorations, like the plush toy dangling from your rearview mirror.

In this chapter, we'll look at how to respond to invitations you get from your friends to use applications; how to tell the worthwhile applications from the worthless ones; how to manage settings and options for the applications you do choose to embrace; and how to remove and block applications you don't like.

And after we've covered all that, we'll finish with a brief roundup of some of Facebook's most popular and entertaining apps.

Applications 101: The Basics

There are certain applications that are part of your Facebook account by default, and most of these have been at least mentioned in the preceding chapters: Notes, Posted Items, Groups, Events, Photos, Videos, and Chat are all basic Facebook applications.

But there are countless other optional applications available to you. Some are made by Facebook, but most are by a host of third-party developers, which allows Facebook to benefit from the individual creativity and inventiveness of many minds.

It's completely up to you which applications (if any) you decide to authorize and how much attention you want to give them. If you really like an application, you can add a box for it to your Profile page. On the other hand, if you don't like an application, you can remove it from your account, and if you find an application especially annoying, you can block it completely so you never get any invitations to use it from your friends.

You can find new applications using Facebook's search tool as well as the Application Directory, which we'll look at later in this chapter. But most likely, before you ever get around to looking for applications, apps will come looking for you, as your friends start sending you invitations to play their favorite games, compare quiz results, accept a gift, or make friends with their dog or ferret.

So we'll start by looking at how applications pop up in your path, and how to accept or reject their overtures.

Responding to Requests from Applications

Back in the *Friends* chapter, we looked at the mechanics of sending and responding to friend requests. But there are other kinds of requests on Facebook, too. For example, when a friend invites you to join a Group, you'll get a Group request, and when someone invites you to an Event, you'll get an Event request.

And last—but certainly not least!—your friends can send you application requests. When a friend of yours wants to interact with you using an application, they'll send you a little message letting you know that you've been invited to participate in whatever the app does.

Like friend requests, application requests show up in the Requests area at the top of the right-hand column on the Home page. You can click on any individual request to go directly to that message on the Requests page—or you can click the total number of requests waiting for you to go to the top of the Requests page.

Each application request looks something like this.

The text on the buttons varies somewhat for each app, but generally the leftmost button says something like Accept or Yes. Clicking this button will take you into the application itself.

The button farthest to the right usually says something like Ignore. Clicking this button makes the request disappear from your Requests page.

For some apps, there may also be a middle button that offers another option, such as viewing information within the application without accepting the request itself.

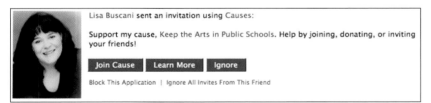

The middle button, Learn More, lets you find out more about the Cause before you decide whether to join it. (For more about the Causes application and how it works, see the section "A Brief Guide to Some Popular Facebook Apps" at the end of this chapter.)

Requests			
🐾 3 friend suggestions		👥 2 friend requests	
📅 7 event invitations		**G** 5 (lil) green patch requests	
💬 19 other requests			

The Requests area on the Home page lets you know how many requests are waiting for you.

NOTE: The first time you accept a request from an application you've never used before, you'll be asked to authorize the application—giving it permission to access your Facebook account for the basic info it needs in order to work. The authorization process is described in the upcoming "Authorizing Applications" section.

TIP: You don't have to respond to application requests right away; there's no time limit or expiration date. So feel free to let them sit for a while if you think you might get around to exploring them later.

How to Block Unwanted App Requests

If you decide that an application just isn't for you, and you don't want to get any more requests from that particular app, you can easily block it from communicating with you in the future. Just below every app request is a Block This Application link. Click that, and you'll get a dialog telling you that in the future the app will be prevented from sending you any requests and from accessing any info about you. (However, you'll still be able to see the app on your friends' pages if they have it displayed.) Click the Block button to confirm.

The Block This Application and Ignore All Invites From This Friend links live just below the Accept and Ignore buttons in an application request.

If you ever change your mind and want to stop blocking an app, you can overturn the restraining order. Just choose Privacy Settings from the Settings menu in the blue bar, and then go to the Applications > Settings page. Find the list of blocked applications at the bottom of the page, and click "remove" next to the app you want to stop blocking. (In other words, you're removing the block, not the application itself.)

How to Block App Requests from Specific Friends

If you have a Facebook friend who sends you lots of requests you aren't interested in, or just don't have time to keep up with—someone who bombards you with 85 cupcakes, Green Patch plants, and vampire bites every day of the week, and doesn't seem to take the hint when you fail to return their largesse—you can choose to ignore all application requests from that particular friend.

Click the Ignore All Invites From This Friend link below any request sent to you by that person. You'll see a dialog asking you to confirm this action, and once you do that, presto—any requests from the friend in question will be automatically ignored before they even reach you.

And don't worry—your friend won't get any kind of notification that you've taken this action, so you don't have to worry about hurting their feelings.

If you change your mind at some point in the future, you can remove your friend's name from the list of people whose requests are ignored by the same process you use to unblock an application, as described in the preceding section. Look for the Ignored Application Inviters list at the bottom of the Privacy Settings > Applications > Settings page, and click "remove" next to the name of the person you'd like to stop ignoring.

Don't Panic!

Facebook apps are social in nature, and they're supposed to be fun—most of them, anyway. So there's no reason to let them stress you out. If you're getting more requests than you can handle, and your mood ring is turning an ugly shade of brown, breathe, relax, and remember that you're not obligated to return Green Patch plants, pet anybody's (fluff)Friend, or get turned into a vampire if that's not your thing. And if your friends are really your friends, they won't judge you for it.

You can remove or block apps, of course, but you can also simply accept gifts without returning them, or click the Ignore button on any requests you don't have time to deal with until you get caught up.

And if you want to give yourself a blank slate, you can clear out all the requests that are piling up by clicking the Ignore All link at the top of the Requests page.

Requests			Ignore All
4 friend suggestions		3 friend requests	
6 event invitations		5 group invitations	
G 7 (lil) green patch		1 rock stars request	

The Ignore All link in the upper-right corner of the box at the top of the Requests page clears out all your current requests.

Authorizing Applications

Authorizing an application is a little bit like adding it to your Friends list—you're giving it permission to access your basic Facebook info, so the two of you can get to know each other a little, and the app knows enough about you to function.

When you access an application for the first time—whether you're accepting a request or clicking on an app you found in search results, the Application Directory, or a link on someone else's profile—you'll get the Allow dialog shown below. Clicking the Allow button authorizes the app and allows you to go ahead with using it.

How to Decide Which Apps Are Worthwhile and Trustworthy

When you get a request from an application you haven't used before, you're presented with a bit of a dilemma. Some Facebook applications are loads of fun, very useful, or both. Others are pointless time-wasters that will annoy you with endless notifications, post inane (and possibly inaccurate) stories to your Wall, and in some cases even pester your friends in your name, without your permission.

So how do you tell the good apps from the bad? How do you decide which ones are worth authorizing and which ones you should kick to the curb?

Fortunately, there's no need to install apps blindly. If you're on the fence, you can do the Facebook equivalent of a background check on an app to help you decide whether you want to authorize it or not.

TIP: As noted back in the *Privacy and Security* chapter, applications are required to respect your privacy settings when accessing your profile info. Once you click the button to authorize an application, it can access any of the information that's available on your profile, with the important exception of your contact info.

Not So Fast, Little App!
Whenever I authorize a new app, the *first* thing I do is change its Wall posting privileges to "Prompt me before publishing any stories" in the Edit Settings dialog. That way I know it won't litter my Wall with several breathless updates before I've had a chance to check it out and decide whether I like it or not.

You can easily access the settings for any app while you're inside it by hovering your mouse over the Settings menu in the blue bar. (See the "Managing Applications" section, later in this chapter, for more info.)

It helps to keep an eye on your Wall, too. I like to visit my Requests page in the morning when I'm having my tea, check out any new apps my friends have sent me, and spend a few minutes playing with my favorites. Then I go check my Wall to see if any stories have been created that I wasn't expecting, and remove them or change their sizes if needed.

> Allowing <u>Word Twist</u> access will le
> friends' info, and <u>ch</u>er content th

Click the name of the application in the Allow dialog to visit the Facebook Page for that app and learn more about it.

The first step in evaluating an app is to take a look at its Facebook Page—every app on Facebook has an informational page with basic information about the app and its makers.

You can access the Page for any app by clicking the name of the app in the request, in the Allow dialog, or anywhere else you see the app's name in blue—which indicates that it's a link to the Page for the app.

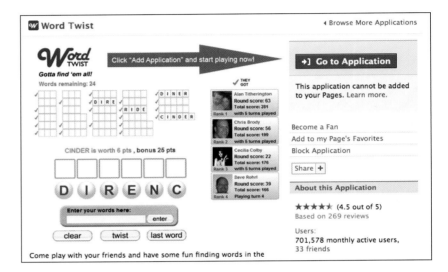

About this Application

★★★★½ (4.5 out of 5)
Based on 269 reviews

Users:
701,578 monthly active users, 33 friends

Categories
Gaming, Just for Fun

This application was **not** developed by Facebook.

The star rating at the top of the "About this Application" box is a pretty good indicator of how its users feel about it.

Once you reach the app's Page, there are several key things to look at:

1. **Star rating.** In the right-hand column toward the top of the Page, you'll see an "About this Application" box, with a rating from one to five stars based on user reviews for the app. That gives you a quick visual gauge of how happy its users are. If the rating is four stars or better, that's a good sign. If it's two stars or below, that may be a red flag.

2. **Friends.** Look for the "Friends Who Have Added this Application" box to see which friends of yours are already using the application. If a lot of friends whose judgment you trust are pictured there, that's a good endorsement. (You can also contact those friends to ask them whether they recommend the app or not.)

3. **User reviews.** Find the Reviews box to read direct feedback from people who've already used this app. If you see a lot of negative reviews, you might want to steer clear—especially if the reviewers give you specific and convincing reasons as to why they're unhappy. On the other hand, glowing praise from fans of the app might convince you that it's worth your time.

4. **Wall and Discussion Board.** You'll also find feedback from the app's users in these areas of the Page. Scan them for recurring complaints or hearty endorsements.

Now you've got some input to go on, and can make an informed decision about whether to app or not to app.

How to Keep from Accidentally Spamming Your Friends

Facebook's third-party apps are viral in nature—they spread through its network by means of friends sending invitations to other friends. In order to grow and flourish, each app needs to persuade its users to send out requests and invitations to people who don't already use the app—and they need to keep existing users coming back, too.

The thing is, there are honorable ways for application developers to accomplish this, and less honorable ones. The most honorable way is, of course, to create such a compellingly entertaining or useful app that people *want* to recommend it to their friends.

But most developers, whether they're striving for quality or not, will hedge their bets a little bit. Very often, when you visit an application, the very first page you see is the one that asks you to send invitations out to your friends.

Needless to say, it can be a bit disorienting to receive a request telling you that you've been sent a fabulous gift, and then when you accept the request you don't see the gift you were sent—all you see is a page of your friends' faces, and a message that exhorts you to send them gifts. And then you have to dig around for a while before you even find the page that shows you the gift you received yourself.

Don't get me wrong—we all know it's more blessed to give than to receive, and there's nothing technically wrong with apps encouraging you to send warm fuzzies to your friends. But you should have the right to bypass that page if you want, and explore the app a little before you decide whether you want to invite your friends to use it, too.

And that's where some developers become less than honorable. Some applications make it very difficult to figure out how to proceed without first sending invitations to one or more of your friends. If you're a new user, or not

TIP: Some apps claim to raise money for charity or political causes—and some have been very effective at it. (Lil) Green Patch, for example, has raised more than $100,000 for the Nature Conservancy at the time of this writing. If you have questions about an app's fundraising claims, check the Page for the app. You can usually find details there about exactly how much money has been raised in the past, and where it's been donated.

Avoid Becoming a Well-Intentioned Pest
When you first start using Facebook apps, it can be difficult to figure out the etiquette. How often should you send your friends requests? How can you tell who wants you to send them Green Patch plants and who doesn't? If you haven't already read "The Fine Art of Not Being Obnoxious," in the *Communicating on Facebook* chapter, you'll find some tips in that section to help you avoid annoying your friends unintentionally.

Requests vs. Notifications

If you're still not clear on the difference between requests and notifications, don't feel bad. It takes a little while to figure out the distinction, and sometimes their functions overlap. (And confusingly, sometimes certain apps may send you the same information as both a request and a notification.)

Here's the basic distinction: Requests usually invite you to take some kind of action, whereas notifications simply tell you that something has happened. (Sometimes notifications may also suggest actions you can take, but in general they're intended as very short news bulletins.)

And of course, requests and notifications show up in different places. Requests appear on the Requests page and are flagged out in the Requests area of the Home page. Notifications turn up on the Notifications page (accessible via the Notifications tab in your Inbox), and you'll see them appear in the little pop-up Notifications menu down in the Applications bar.

As an example, when someone sends you a gift using an app like Send Cupcakes, you'll get a request asking you to accept the cupcake (and authorize the app if you've never used it before)—and then you can choose a cupcake to send back to your friend if you like. On the other hand, when a friend accepts a gift you've sent them, the news will come to you as a notification rather than a request—because there's no additional action you need to take at that point.

careful, and you're accessing one of these apps for the first time, it's possible to wind up spamming a whole slew of your friends without meaning to.

Facebook used to get a lot of complaints about this problem, so a while back they instituted a firm rule that apps are *always* required to let you opt out of inviting your friends. Somewhere on the invitations page there has to be a Skip button—or other navigational elements, like tabs or buttons—that will let you go on into the app without inviting anyone else to use it. If the app *doesn't* have that, it's in clear violation of Facebook's rules, and if enough users report it, Facebook will deactivate it until the developers bring it into compliance.

An example of a Skip button (over on the right-hand side) on the invitations page for a gift-giving application

So—know your rights as an app user and don't send invitations to your friends unless you want to, and you've decided that the app is worthy of their attention. If you hit an invitations page and you're not ready to send out any invitations, look around until you find a button or link that says *Skip* (or other words to that effect), or some tabs or buttons that let you go to other pages within the app.

And if you find an app that's violating the rules, use the Report link at the bottom of the page to let Facebook know about it.

The navigational tabs at the top of the Monty Python Gifts application let you click to other pages in the app without sending invitations first.

Notifications from Apps

In addition to sending you requests, applications you've authorized can send you notifications. Just like the notifications you get when someone accepts a friend request, writes on your Wall, or comments on a photo of you, notifications from applications are little announcements that let you know about something. You might get a notification that a friend has "thrown mashed potatoes at you" using SuperPoke, or beaten your score in a word game you both play, or dedicated a song to you using the iLike music app.

You'll see these notifications appear in the little number balloon on the Notifications icon in the Applications bar, and on the Notifications page itself.

> ❄ Lori Dana threw a new snowball at you! Catch it! or Throw one back! 6:35am   ✕

An example of a notification from an application, on the Notifications page

Blocking Unwanted Notifications

If an application is pestering you with too many notifications, or with notifications you don't find interesting, you can take away its notification privileges.

On the Notifications page, along the right-hand column, you'll see a series of checkboxes for applications that have sent you notifications in the past. Deselecting the checkbox for any application in the list will muzzle it from sending you notifications in the future (unless and until you select its checkbox again).

Some applications also give you more specific controls that let you decide what kinds of notifications they send you.

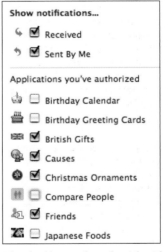

The checkboxes along the right side of the Notifications page let you decide whether specific apps are allowed to send you notifications.

The options within the British Gifts application (found by clicking its Options tab) let you distinguish between different kinds of notifications.

Managing Applications

Facebook gives you a healthy amount of control over the applications you use. If you don't like the stories an application is posting to your Wall, you can take away its posting privileges. If you decide an app isn't for you after you've been using it for a while, you can send it packing by deauthorizing it.

On the positive side, if you really like a particular app, you can feature it as a box on your profile, or even give it its own tab.

And you can do all of these things from one central location on Facebook: the Applications page.

facebook	Home	Profile	Friends	Inbox 4		Dave Awl	Settings	Logout

Application Settings - Recently Used

Displaying 55 applications you have used in the past month.   Show: Recently Used

G (Lil) Green Patch	Edit Settings	About	X
(fluff)Friends	Edit Settings	About	X
80's	Edit Settings	About	X
AD Addicted to Arrested Development	Edit Settings	About	X

The Applications Page

Use the Settings pop-up menu in the blue bar to visit the Applications page.

There are three easy ways to get to Facebook's Applications page:

- Hover your mouse above the word *Settings* in the blue bar, and then choose Application Settings from the pop-up menu;
- Click the Edit link in the pop-up Applications menu in the Applications bar; or
- Click the Edit link in the Applications area of the right-hand column on the Home page.

Once you're there, you can use the Show pop-up menu to choose which of your applications are displayed, so that you can home in on certain categories, such as applications you've used recently, applications that are allowed to post on your Wall, and so forth.

How to Edit the Settings for an Application

For each application that's listed on the Applications page, you'll see an Edit Settings link that opens the Settings dialog for that app, as shown below.

Edit Pieces of Flair Settings

| Wall | Profile | Bookmark | Additional Permissions |

- ○ Allow Pieces of Flair to publish one-line stories automatically, but prompt me for larger stories.
- ● Prompt me before publishing any stories from Pieces of Flair.
- ○ Never publish any stories from Pieces of Flair.
- ○ Allow Pieces of Flair to publish specific story sizes automatically without prompting.

Okay

The four tabs in this dialog give you a variety of useful controls. The Wall tab shown above, for example, lets you specify whether the app is allowed to post stories to your Wall, whether you need to approve them first, and how detailed they can be.

How to Control Who Can See a Specific Application

The Profile tab in the Edit Settings dialog contains a Privacy pop-up menu that lets you control who is allowed to see that specific application. Choosing Custom from the menu opens a dialog that lets you specify Friend Lists or Networks, as explained in the *Privacy and Security* chapter.

What Are "Additional Permissions"?

The Additional Permissions tab in the Edit Settings dialog has two checkboxes.

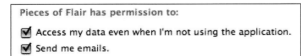

Pieces of Flair has permission to:
- ☑ Access my data even when I'm not using the application.
- ☑ Send me emails.

- ■ "Access my data even when I'm not using the application" means that if you're logged out of Facebook, a friend can still use an app to interact with you, such as SuperPoking you or starting a word game with you.
- ■ "Send me emails" means the app is allowed to send notifications to your e-mail address.

The Show menu on the Applications page lets you choose which categories of applications are displayed on the page.

If you're already inside a particular app, you don't have to go to the Applications page to change its settings. A handy temporary link to its settings appears in the Settings menu while you're in the app, and then disappears when you exit.

The Privacy control in the Edit Settings dialog

How to Remove Applications You Don't Like

Clicking the X at the far right side of the listing for any application opens a dialog that lets you remove (deauthorize) or block the app in question.

The Boxes Tab

If you really like an application, you can add a box for the app to your Profile page. Most of these boxes will appear on the Boxes tab of your profile (although some apps give you the option of displaying their boxes on the Wall and Info tabs instead of the Boxes tab).

You can think of the Boxes tab as being the rec room of your profile—a place you can decorate with your own mixture of silly and serious apps that express your personality. Friends can drop by your Boxes tab to play games with you; check out your taste in books, movies, and films; learn about the causes you support; or see what gifts your other friends have been sending you lately.

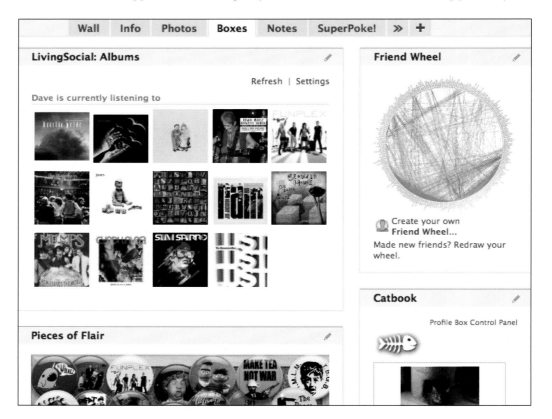

Adding a Box to Your Profile

If and when you decide you like an application well enough to add its box to your profile, there are two ways to do it: from the Applications page, or from within the app itself. To do the former, go to the Applications page, find the application you want, and click the Edit Settings link. In the dialog, click the Profile tab. Then click the Add link next to the word *Box*. To remove a box, follow the same steps and click the word *Remove*.

Edit Goodreads Books Settings

Wall	Profile	Bookmark	Additional Permissions

Box: Available (add)

Some (but not all) apps give you the option of placing them on your Wall tab instead of your Boxes tab. It's up to you to decide where you'd rather display the box. If you choose the Wall tab, your app will be displayed a little more prominently, in the left-hand column on the tab that your friends are most likely to visit. On the other hand, if you place the box on the Boxes tab, you'll generally get a larger box that displays more content.

TIP: Just like the boxes on your Wall tab, the boxes displayed on your Boxes tab can be rearranged by dragging them to their desired locations. See the *Signing Up and Setting Up Your Profile* chapter for an example of this.

Adding Extra Tabs to Your Profile

We've already talked about the four tabs that appear on your Profile page by default (assuming you have the necessary content to make them all appear): Wall, Info, Photos, and Boxes. But you can also add optional extra tabs for your favorite applications. If you're a heavy SuperPoke user, for example, you can give SuperPoke its own dedicated tab. Same for Pieces of Flair, (Lil) Green Patch, Causes, and many others. (See the facing page for an example.)

To add a tab, click the plus (+) button to the right of the other tabs at the top of your profile. Then choose the app you'd like to promote to its own tab from the pop-up list that appears. (If you don't see the app you want in the menu, you can type its name in the search field to see if it's available.)

TIP: You can rearrange the order of your tabs by dragging them. But note that only two extra tabs will appear above your profile; any others you create are shifted to an overflow menu marked with a >> symbol, right next to the plus button.

You can access the options for an application's box by clicking its Pencil icon. The menu includes the options to move the box to the Wall tab or remove the box from your profile.

TIP: Boxes you choose to display on your Wall tab are visible on your Info tab as well. (It's kind of a two-for-one deal.) Also, there's a limit to how many boxes can be displayed on your Wall tab—extras will be automatically bumped back to the Boxes tab.

The menu for adding an extra tab to your profile

NOTE: The option to give an app its own tab isn't available for every application on Facebook—that capability has to have been built into the app by its developers. But if you love an app enough to want to give it extra emphasis on your profile, it's worth taking a minute to try adding a tab for it—the worst that will happen is that you'll get a message telling you the app you're looking for isn't tab friendly just yet.

TIP: Basic Facebook apps like Notes, Posted Items, Groups, Events, Photos, and Videos are bookmarked for you by default.

Bookmarking Your Apps

You can create handy shortcuts to access your favorite apps quickly by bookmarking them. Apps you've chosen to bookmark appear in the pop-up menu in the Applications bar as well as in the Applications area in the right-hand column on the Home page.

Adding Bookmarks

To bookmark an app, go to the Applications page, click Edit Settings, and then click the Bookmark tab. Once you select the Bookmark checkbox, the app will appear in your list of bookmarks.

Applications

Drag to reorder.   Edit | Find More

- Twitter
- Pieces of Flair
- (Lil) Green Patch
- Sea Garden
- Catbook
- SuperPoke!

- Send Good Karma
- Geo Challenge
- Page Manager
- Groups

Bookmarks as they appear in the pop-up Applications menu

Edit British Gifts Settings

Wall   Profile   **Bookmark**

☑ Bookmark British Gifts

Okay

Reorganizing Bookmarks

You can change the order in which your bookmarks appear by dragging them in the Applications pop-up menu. Move the ones you use most often to the top, so that they're easy to find when you need them. When you rearrange the order of your bookmarks in the Applications pop-up menu, the bookmarks shown in the right-hand column of the Home page also change to reflect the new arrangement.

Bookmark Buttons

Facebook lets you pick your six favorite bookmarked applications to appear as buttons in the Applications bar. Whichever six apps are listed first in the Applications pop-up menu—the ones that appear above the line—are the ones that will appear as buttons next to the pop-up menu.

Finding Apps: The Application Directory

If you'd like to browse for interesting new apps without waiting for a friend to send you a request, Facebook makes it easy. You can go app hunting any time you want using the Application Directory.

To access the directory, click the pop-up Applications menu in the Applications bar. At the top of the menu, click the Find More link, which will take you directly to the Application Directory.

Application Directory   Search Applications

| **Applications You May Like** | **Most Active Users** | **Newest** |

MyCalendar
By MyCalender

17,679,976 monthly active users — 113 friends — 26 reviews

Applications by Language:

English (US)

Browse Applications:

For Facebook Profiles

Top Friends
By Slide, Inc.

Own your profile with Top Friends! Now you can CUSTOMIZE your Top Friends Profile! Choose your skin, add music and more. Give and receive exclusive awards, show off your mood and keep tabs on the people you really care about with Top Friends News!

16,230,803 monthly active users — 84 friends — 1,162 reviews

Likeness
By RockYou!

Find out who you're like! Compare yourself with friends and movie stars like Angelina Jolie, Jessica Alba, Keira Knightley, and many more. Can you find a perfect

All
Alerts
Business
Chat
Classified
Dating
Education
Events
Fashion

The default page for the directory shows you a selection of apps that Facebook thinks you might like, based on actions you've taken in the past. But using the tabs across the top, you can also view the most popular apps on Facebook (Most Active Users) or the newest apps in the directory.

The categories along the right side of the page let you browse apps that relate to (for example) fashion, dating, business, music, politics, gaming, and many other niches.

You can use the search field at the top of the Application Directory to search for applications by name (if you're looking for an app you already know the name of) or by keyword (if you're looking for apps related to cats or cooking or Lithuania or kayaking, for example).

A Brief Guide to Some Popular Facebook Apps

There are thousands of apps on Facebook, and it would be impossible to do more than scratch the surface of them—so the roundup that follows is shamelessly subjective and arbitrary. My goal here isn't to present a definitive catalog of Facebook's best apps, but just to show you a little of the range and variety of apps that are available, and encourage you to do some exploring to find your own favorites.

Culture-Sharing Apps

One of the best parts of life on Facebook is the ability to share what you're reading, listening to, and watching with your friends, and keep track of what's on their cultural radar as well.

There are lots of apps that make it easy to display your current recommendations on your profile, and find out about new books, music, and films by your favorite artists (as well as new discoveries).

iLike is a perfect example of this. Although iLike wasn't developed by Facebook, it's the closest thing Facebook has to an official music application. Posting the iLike box on your profile lets you display a selection of your favorite musicians and a playlist of songs you like.

iLike's Home page (shown on the facing page) helps you keep track of the artists you're a fan of, check out their new releases, find out when they're touring in your area, and make plans to meet up at concerts with friends. You can also use iLike to dedicate songs and videos to your friends, and challenge your friends to music trivia quizzes.

LivingSocial: Albums is another useful music app that's geared to showing off your album collection. You can display, rate, and review the albums you're currently listening to, as well as your old favorites.

For book lovers, **Visual Bookshelf** lets you display the covers of books you're currently reading, books you've already read, and books you want to read. You can rate and review books, and check out what your friends are reading.

If you're already a member of the Goodreads book-sharing site, you'll find that the **Goodreads** app conveniently syncs your book list to the Goodreads box you can place on your Facebook profile.

The **Flixter Movies** app is geared toward movie buffs. It lets you catalog and rate the movies you've seen, and compare your rankings with those of your friends. From the app's Home page you can also watch trailers, check show-times for local theaters, play film trivia games, and more.

The **Addicted to …** application lets you pick your favorite show (choose from a diverse selection that includes *Lost*, *The Simpsons*, *The Colbert Report*, *Arrested Development*, *House*, *Heroes*, *Sex and the City*, *Doctor Who*, and many more) and announce your addiction to the world. You can use the app to display favorite quotes from the show on your profile, discuss the show with fellow fans, and try to beat your friends' scores on trivia quizzes.

Friendship Apps

As your circle of Facebook friends grows, you can use Facebook apps to display their faces, organize them, chart their relationships to each other, and even rank them as "top friends," à la MySpace.

The **Gridview** and **Entourage** applications let you create collages of your friends' profile pictures, so you can see their faces on your own profile (above and beyond the handful that show up in Facebook's Friends box).

Top Friends takes the selective approach and lets you display just the upper echelon of your Friends list.

Friend Statistics crunches the numbers on your friends and tells you how they fit into various demographic categories—by political leanings, by age, by gender, and even by zodiac sign.

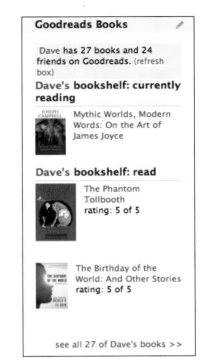

The profile box for the Goodreads application

The Addicted to Arrested Development box

Friend Wheel creates a circular display of your friends' names, and then draws links between them to show how they're socially connected to each other—creating an interesting graphical portrait of your social network.

Self-Expression Apps

Decking out your profile to express your personality is a huge part of the Facebook experience, and there are plenty of creative and engaging apps to help you do that.

Pieces of Flair lets you collect and display small round buttons on a virtual bulletin board. You can spend hours obsessively browsing through the catalog of thousands of pins created by the Pieces of Flair users, and then arranging them into the perfect expression of your personality. You can even create your own button images and send them to your friends.

Friend Wheel

Create your own
Friend Wheel...
Made new friends? Redraw your wheel.

The Friend Wheel app is a graphic depiction of your circle of friends.

The **Stickerz** and **Bumper Sticker** applications work similarly, but instead of buttons you collect and create stickers.

10 Second Interview treats you like a rock star, letting you answer a series of short interview questions and displaying the resulting Q & A session on your profile.

The **Art** application lets you pick out a few of your favorite paintings to display on your profile.

10 Second Interview

Are you a glass half full or glass half empty person?

(Answer)   Skip | Skip Forever

Show My Answers | Hide My Answers

Want this? Add it!

⏱A 10 Second Interview with Dave Awl
What are three words that sum you up?
Precious little pumpkin.
What album could you listen to every day for the rest of your life?
The Rise and Fall of Ziggy Stardust and the Spiders from Mars
What one possession would you save in a fire?
A magic box that contains a replacement for everything I own.

10 Second Interview asks you a bunch of silly questions. You get to supply the silly answers.

Warm Fuzzy–Sending Apps

In addition to the basic gift-giving apps that were covered in the *Communicating on Facebook* chapter, there are some apps that add interesting twists to the gift-giving process.

Hatching Eggs lets you send a gift to a friend that arrives as an egg. You pick what's inside the egg—choose from plants, animals, mythical creatures, you name it—and over over several days the egg gradually hatches in your friend's profile to reveal the surprise waiting inside. You can enclose a message with your hatching gift, too.

Growing Gifts and **Water Globe Gifts** work similarly to Hatching Eggs, except that for Growing Gifts, your gift appears as a plant that gradually blooms in a clay pot, and for Water Globe Gifts, your gift gradually appears in a glass ball as the snow that obscures it clears away.

If you'd like to buy your friends a (strictly virtual) drink, applications like **Booze Mail** and **Pass a Drink** let you treat them to their favorite tipple. (Nonalcoholic beverages like green tea and hot cider are options, too.)

Family and Genealogy Apps

You can display your family ties on your profile using the **We're Related** app, which lets you find and display your relatives who are on Facebook, and gradually build your family tree. **Family Tree** works similarly.

The **Circle of Moms** application creates a community of mothers on Facebook who share advice and recommendations, and allows them to create secure and private Kid Profiles for their children.

Wall Apps

Facebook has several popular apps that attempt to provide a more full-featured version of Facebook's Wall, offering additional formatting controls and the ability to post the same content on multiple friends' Walls at once. **SuperWall**, **FunSpace** (formerly known as FunWall), and **Advanced Wall** all fall into this category.

> **TIP:** Personally, after experimenting with several Wall apps, I removed them all and decided that the standard-issue Facebook Wall is the only Wall I need. The Wall apps resulted in lots of mass-forwarded posts appearing on my Wall, which mostly felt like social spam (imagine the worst mass-forwarded "joke" e-mails you get from your friends with the worst taste, and you'll have some idea of what I'm talking about).

Andy Dixon's egg is hatching!   click **Lori Dana's** egg hatched a piglet.

Left, an egg in the process of hatching, and right, a fully hatched gift

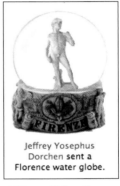

Jeffrey Yosephus Dorchen **sent a** Florence water globe.

A Water Globe gift

Circle of Moms is a resource for mothers on Facebook.

Activism

The **Causes** application makes it easy to support the causes you believe in. Choose from a diverse selection of charitable and political organizations whose goals you believe in. Once you click the link to "join" a cause, you can recruit other supporters and help raise donations for the organizations you've chosen to support.

Travel and Geography

If you'd like to test your travel smarts, **Geo Challenge** is a lively animated video game that tests you on your knowledge of world geography. Score points by locating cities on a map, identifying countries by their borders, and correctly recognizing national flags. Compare your points with your friends' and work your way up through the scoring levels as you learn.

You can show off your globe-trotting adventures with the **Cities I've Visited** and **Where I've Been** applications. Both apps create an interactive map for your profile that displays the cities, towns, and countries you've visited in your travels, allowing you to compare your journeys with those of your friends.

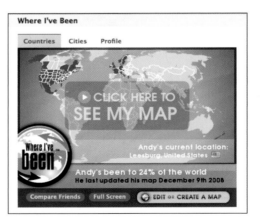

Profiles for Pets

Let's face it—those of us with animal companions think of them as our friends. So it's only natural that lots of Facebook users have the urge to create Facebook accounts for their cats, dogs, ferrets, and other nonhuman room-mates. But technically, these are against Facebook's rules (because you're not supposed to create an account on someone else's behalf), so they can be deactivated as "fake profiles" if Facebook discovers them.

Kiwi

will find a way to make a toy out of that thing you dropped. Just watch him! (edit)

Family:	you (remove)
Breed:	Domestic Shorthair/Tabby
Gender:	Male
Birthday:	April 6, 2005
Loved Since:	2005
Hometown:	Chicago, Illinois, United States (edit)
Activities:	Birdwatching, morning floor ballet, slow blinking, mousie fishing, SBD toxic emissions, drowning all manner of things in the water bowl, lap snuggling, cave lurking, hiding from guests, missing my adoptive brother Mr. Blue, and (formerly) wrestling, chasing, and gnawing on Mr. Blue all day long before Mr. Blue went to feline heaven. (edit)
Favourite Furniture:	The underneath of the foldout love seat, and the crow's nest of the cat tree. (edit)
Favourite Treats:	Organic catnip. (edit)
About Me:	Adopted from Tree House Animal Foundation in Andersonville. Rescued after being found on a golf course at one day old and miraculously nursed to health by the fabulous Tree House staff! Read the story of my adoption here: http://tinyurl.com/bedrk (edit)

Pet Him!
Change Profile Picture
Edit Profile Information
Change Status Message
Invite Friends For Him
Delete Profile

Add as a Friend

For You ▼   Add

Kiwi's Friends

26 total   See All

Minifeed

ⓘ Kiwi will find a way to make a toy out of that thing you dropped. Just watch him!   2:36pm November 28th, 2008

✕

Photos

11 total   Add Photo | See All

Fortunately, there's a great set of related apps that come to the rescue. You can create a profile for your cat on **Catbook** (shown above) or for your dog on **Dogbook**, listing their favorite activities and interests.

Your pet's profile comes complete with its own Wall and status update, and the ability to make friends with other pets and human beings. In addition to Catbook and Dogbook, there's also **Ferretbook**, **Horsebook**, **Rodentbook**, and **Fishbook**. (One can only hope that Reptilebook is in development.)

Virtual Pet and Gardening Apps

If creating profiles for your real-world pets isn't enough for you, don't worry—there are plenty of opportunities to nurture virtual plants and animals on Facebook, too.

The wildly popular **(Lil) Green Patch** app is a successful blend of gift-giving, poking, self-expression, and environmental activism. (Lil) Green Patch gives you a small garden plot to display on your profile. Friends can send each other plants (some rendered as fanciful plant-headed children) to grow in their gardens.

Plants and plant-headed children live happily together in the (Lil) Green Patch.

The Otter character from the Sea Garden application

The plants can also be sold in the Green Patch Marketplace in exchange for points (called Green Bucks), which can then be used to buy decorative gifts you bestow on a friend's garden or display in your own. Friends can also tend each other's patches—each patch displays the faces of the most recent gardeners to stop by and take care of it. Best of all, (Lil) Green Patch raises money for the Nature Conservancy to help protect rainforests.

Sea Garden is similar to (Lil) Green Patch, but instead of plants, friends send each other whales, dolphins, stingrays, and other sea creatures. Friends can also hide gifts inside each other's treasure chests, and send each other messages in bottles. Sea Garden helps raise funds for ocean protection organizations, including the Surfrider foundation.

The **(fluff)Friends** app lets you choose a virtual pet to take care of and display on your profile. You can give your (fluff)Friend a name and a personality, buy it treats and habitats in the (fluff)Friend gift shop, and even enter it into races against your friends' (fluff)Friends.

Hatchlings works kind of like an Easter egg hunt—in fact, this app started out as an Easter egg game, but proved popular enough to take on a life beyond the holiday. Look for eggs in the profiles of friends who have Hatchlings installed, and click the eggs to add them to your basket. You can trade the eggs with friends, or keep them and watch them hatch into virtual pets.

myFarm, which raises money for hunger relief, gives you a plot of land on which to grow virtual tomatoes, strawberries, wheat, corn, and other crops. You can watch your crops gradually grow and harvest them each day. Friends can send each other various kinds of fruit trees, as well as animated horses, goats, cows, and chickens to add life to their farms. The crops and fruit you harvest earn "myFarm cash" that can be used to buy barns, farmhouses, and other additions to outfit your growing farm.

Word Games

Word games are an ever-popular pastime both online and off, and Facebook has a thriving lexicon of them.

A gray horse grazes next to a blossoming orange tree in the myFarm app.

The most famous of these is **Wordscraper**, which began life as an online version of Scrabble called Scrabulous that quickly became the most popular game on Facebook. Unfortunately, the developers of Scrabulous didn't own the rights to Scrabble, and after a much-publicized legal dispute they were reluctantly forced to reinvent the application as Wordscraper, with a somewhat different look and feel.

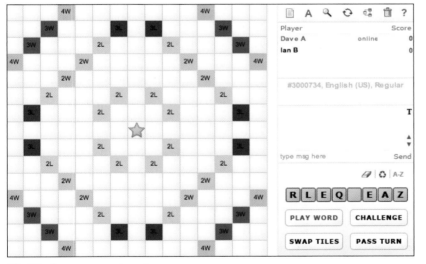

The Wordscraper game board

There's now an official, authorized **Scrabble** application available on Facebook as well, but neither it nor Wordscraper draws as many players as Scrabulous did at the height of its popularity.

Other popular Facebook word games include **Word Twist**, which lets you challenge a friend to see who can create the most words out of a series of random letters. You earn points for speed as well as the length of the words you find. In **Scramble**, the goal is to find words in a grid of letters, playing solo or against friends. **Pathwords** is similar, but keeps things active by adding new letters to the board as you play, and removing letters you've used.

The Scramble word grid

The Vampires app lets you put the bite on your friends.

Other Games

Facebook is a never-ending arcade that lets you play every kind of game imaginable: from card games to board games and beyond. You can play poker with your pals using the **Texas HoldEm Poker** app, knock down the pins with **Bowling Buddies,** match wits with your friends using the animated **Who Has the Biggest Brain?** game, or develop superhuman powers with **My Heroes Ability.**

PackRat is a highly addictive game that appeals to the obsessive collector in everyone: It involves competing against your friends to assemble complete sets of illustrated cards.

If you like role-playing (and have a bit of a gothic streak), **Vampires** lets you put the bite on your friends, scoring points for every pal you turn into a bloodthirsty bat. The **WereWolves** and **Zombies** apps work similarly, and you can even stake out the Van Helsing role using the **Slayers** application.

And for the medievalists in the crowd, **Knighthood** allows you to build a feudal kingdom by acquiring vassals, and raiding other lords and ladies while fortifying your own defenses.

Apps for Bloggers

If you've got a blog outside of Facebook, there are plenty of ways to import and promote your blog's content on Facebook. As discussed in the *Wall, Status, and News Feeds* chapter, you can use Facebook's Import function to turn your blog posts into Facebook Notes automatically. But there are some great third-party apps for bloggers, too.

Simplaris Blogcast allows you to display your recent blog posts in a self-contained box on your profile. Posts can be imported from your blog either manually or automatically, giving you control over which blog posts you display on your profile, and when.

The **NetworkedBlogs** app (formerly Blog Networks) helps you promote your blog by adding it to a directory of Facebook blogs and connecting it to your friends who have blogs of their own. Using this app allows you to display a blogroll of your favorite blogs on your profile, so that you and your friends can help steer traffic to each other.

Live Blog lets you create blog entries to post on your profile with advanced formatting that goes beyond what the Notes application offers—including the ability to embed YouTube videos in your posts.

For Students

Courses 2.0 lets you post your current class schedule on your profile and compare your schedule with your friends' to see who will be in your classes. You can also use this app to network with classmates, form study groups, and buy and sell used textbooks.

The Facebook Toolbar for Firefox

If you use Firefox as your Web browser, Facebook has a nifty toolbar you can install that gives you quick access to much of Facebook's functionality even when you don't have Facebook itself open in your browser.

You can find the toolbar easily by searching the Application Directory or the blue bar for *Facebook toolbar*. (You'll also find it in the For Your Desktop category in the Application Directory.)

Click on the listing and follow the easy instructions to install the toolbar.

Once the toolbar is installed, you'll be able to see at a glance your current number of new pokes, friend requests, and Event and Group invitations. The toolbar also includes a handy Facebook Share button, a search field, a Home button, a Quick Links menu that gives you access to key Facebook pages, and a status update field (not shown above).

8

Photos and Videos

Photos are a huge part of life on Facebook. With more than 700 million photos uploaded each month, Facebook is the Web's largest photo-sharing site—bigger than Flickr or Photobucket.

Uploading your photos to Facebook does more than just give you a place to put them. Photos posted on Facebook get attention, because sharing photos on Facebook is an active process. Facebook's News Feeds ensure that when you post photos on Facebook, other people will know about it and check them out.

Facebook is also an ideal place to host and share original videos, which benefit the same way photos do from Facebook's News Feeds.

In this chapter, we'll start by looking at the various ways to view photos and videos on Facebook, and then we'll cover how to upload, organize, and tag your own photos and videos.

And because Facebook photos and videos are great vehicles for promoting creative projects, events, and causes, we'll talk a little about how you can use them to help get attention for whatever you've got that needs an audience.

Sharing Photos on Facebook

In a sense, posting photos on Facebook is the opposite of the slide shows my older relatives used to put on when I was a kid. With a slide show, you'd invite everyone to gather in one place to look at some photos together. With Facebook, on the other hand, the photos you post seek out their audience, finding their way to your friends in all sorts of different places.

Facebook's News Feeds and notifications mean that when you publish photos on Facebook, people notice. And because each photo you post has its own comments thread, you'll get feedback too, as lively conversations spring up about each picture. (Maybe even livelier than the conversations my aunts and uncles used to have at those old-fashioned slide shows.)

Facebook gives you a bunch of useful tools to help you post your photos easily and organize them into albums. But before we talk about posting photos, let's look at how you can view your friends' photos on Facebook. That way, when you're ready to upload your own photos, you'll have a sense of how and where they'll be visible to others.

Viewing Photos

There are three easy ways to view photos on Facebook: check them out via the News Feed on the Home page, browse them from within the Photos application, or drop by a particular friend's profile to see all their photos.

The News Feed's Photos Tab

Clicking the Photos tab on the Home page brings up a chronological listing of photos posted by your friends—or photos in which at least one of your friends was tagged—with the most recent stories on top. You can click on individual photos, or the names of photo albums, to comment on them.

What Is This Thing Called "Tagging"?

Each time you upload a new photo or video to Facebook, you have the option to *tag* the people who appear in it. Tagging involves clicking on the faces of the people in the picture, and then choosing their names from a pop-up list of your friends. Anyone you tag will get a notification from Facebook, announcing that a new photo or video of them has been posted, so they can go take a look at it.

Tagging someone also means that a story will appear on their Wall about the photo or video, and News Feed stories may appear on the Home pages of their friends as well.

You can tag people who aren't on Facebook, too, and Facebook will send a notification message to the e-mail address you specify for them.

Tags can be added and removed at any time. And you always have the option to remove your own name from any photos or videos where you've been tagged. See "Detagging Photos and Videos," later in this chapter.

The Photos Application

Facebook's Photos app is its central hub for both viewing and posting photos. Photos is one of the basic Facebook applications that are part of your account by default, so you should find it already bookmarked in the Applications pop-up menu and the Applications area of the Home page.

TIP: If for any reason the Photos app is missing from your bookmarks, you can restore the bookmark by going to the Applications page, opening the Edit Settings dialog for the Photos app, and clicking the Profile tab. If the Photos app is missing from your authorized apps, you can find it by searching, just like any other app, and then reauthorize it.

Photos My Photos	Photos of Me	Help

Recent Albums	**Mobile Uploads**	**Tagged Friends**

Displaying 1–20 of 1418 friends' recent albums.

When you enter the Photos app, the first thing you'll see is the Recent Photos tab, which displays your friends' recently posted or updated photo albums. Clicking the Mobile Uploads tab shows you photos your friends have recently uploaded from their phones or other mobile devices. The Tagged Friends tab rounds up the photos in which your friends have been recently tagged.

You can also view your own photos by clicking the My Photos link at the top of the screen, and any photos in which you've been tagged recently by clicking the Photos of Me link.

Friends' Profiles

If you want to view photos of a particular friend, you can swing by their profile, where there are a few different ways to access their photos. The most obvious is to click the Photos tab, if it's visible.

The Photos tab shows you photos in which your friend has been tagged in the top part of the page, and your friend's photo albums in the bottom part. (And of course, your own Photos tab works the same way for your own photos.)

The Photos box

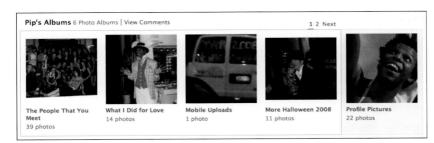

If the Photos box is visible on your friend's profile (on either the Wall tab or the Boxes tab, depending on where they've chosen to place it), you can click the See All link to go the page that shows all of their photo albums.

If the Photos box isn't displayed, you can click the View Photos of *Name* link just under your friend's profile picture, which will take you to the same selection of photos as the Boxes tab.

Click the link under a friend's profile picture to see their photos.

Adding Photos

Uploading your photos to Facebook is a quick and painless process. Facebook gives you a number of tools to make it easy, including a Java-based uploader that allows you to post entire sets of photos at once, and an optional application you can use to export photos from iPhoto.

NOTE: If you've already created an album that you'd like to add photos to, you can bypass this step. See the "Editing and Adding Photos to Existing Albums" section. And if you're uploading from your mobile phone, you can upload to the automatically created Mobile Uploads album.

Creating an Album

Facebook photos are organized into albums, so before you upload any photos to Facebook you need to create at least one album. Start by going to the Photos application, and then click the Create a Photo Album button in the upper-right corner of the page.

Photos My Photos | Photos of Me | Help	+ Create a Photo Album
Recent Albums Mobile Uploads Tagged Friends	

NOTE: If you've already created an album that you'd like to add photos to, you can bypass this step. See the "Editing and Adding Photos to Existing Albums" section.

On the Create Album page, the first step is to name the Album—pick something descriptive. Next, type the location where the shots were taken. (This step is optional.) Then, in the Description field, you can type some descriptive or introductory text that will appear on the main page for the album you're creating. You can think of it as a caption that applies to the group of photos as a whole (as opposed to the captions for each photo that you'll be creating later on).

Finally, use the Privacy menu to decide who will be allowed to see the photos in this album. If the photos you're posting are promotional, then you'll want to choose Everyone to give them the widest possible audience. On the other hand, if they're personal—photos of a family gathering, for example—you might want to limit the album to Only Friends, or even choose the Custom setting to restrict access to a particular Friend List.

Once you've completed those steps, you're ready to click the Create Album button.

Uploading Photos

Once you've created your album, you'll arrive at the Upload Photos screen. A dialog will appear asking you to authorize Facebook's photo uploader Java applet, which makes it easy to upload multiple photos quickly and easily. Click the Trust button to grant the necessary access to your hard drive.

If you prefer not to authorize the applet, or you have trouble getting it to work, you can choose the Simple Uploader, which works without Java. The downside to the Simple Uploader is that you'll have to browse for each individual photo you want to add to the album—which isn't a problem if you're only adding a few but can be a real pain if you're uploading dozens of pics.

Using the Java Uploader

If you decide to use the photo uploader Java applet, once you've clicked Trust to authorize it you can use the left side of the uploader window to navigate to the folder on your hard drive that contains the photos you want to upload.

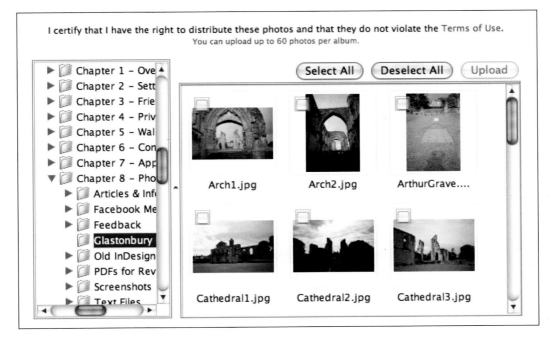

If you want to upload everything that's in the folder you've navigated to, you can take the easy route and just click the Select All button at the top. If you're only uploading some of the contents, you can select the checkboxes next to the individual photos you do want to upload. (Or, if it's easier, click Select All and then deselect the files you don't want to upload.)

Once you've made your selection, click the Upload button to proceed. A dialog will open showing you the progress of your upload, and when it's complete, a message will appear telling you the upload was successful. Click OK.

Using the Simple Uploader

If you prefer to use the Simple Uploader, you can access it using the link at the bottom of the dialog for the Java Uploader.

Trouble uploading photos? Try the Simple Uploader.

TIP: You can also upload photos and videos directly from your mobile phone. See the *Going Mobile* chapter for more info.

Once you've opened the Simple Uploader, use the Browse buttons to navigate to each of the first five photos you'd like to upload. (If you have more than five photos, you can upload them in separate batches.)

> **Photos:**
> You can upload JPG, GIF or PNG files.
>
> Browse...
> Browse...

Once you've specified the photos you want to upload, select the checkbox to confirm that you have the right to post these photos, and that they don't violate Facebook's rules. Then click the Upload Photos button to proceed.

> ☐ **I certify that I have the right to distribute these photos and that they do not violate the Terms of Use.**
>
> **Upload Photos**   or   Cancel
>
> The file size limit 5 MB. If your upload does not work, try uploading a smaller picture.

Using the iPhoto Exporter

Facebook makes it easy to upload photos from iPhoto using the iPhoto Exporter app, which you can find by searching the Application Directory or using the convenient links at the bottom of the dialogs for the Java and Simple uploaders.

> Application: **Facebook Exporter for iPhoto**   View Application
> Developer: Facebook
> Description: Tag, caption, and export photos from your iPhoto library directly to Facebook.
> Users: 314,220 monthly active users – 19 friends

Editing Photo Information

Once you've uploaded your photos, you'll arrive at the Edit Photos screen, where you can add or change the basic info for each individual photo.

Type a caption in the caption box that will appear on the page with the photo it applies to. Click the button that says, "This is the album cover," next to the photo you'd like to appear on the Albums page as the icon for this album. You can also select the "Delete this photo" checkbox to remove the photo from the album, and use the "Move to" menu to transfer it to a different album (assuming you've already created others to choose from).

clicking the Add More tab, which will take you back to the uploader. You can click the Edit Photos tab to return to the screen where you can change captions and other attributes at any time, and clicking the Edit Info tab takes you to the screen where you can change the description, location, and privacy settings for the album.

Additional Photo Controls

On the Album page, click any photo to go to the page for that photo. Down at the bottom of the page, you'll see some additional controls. You can change the photo's orientation using the rotate buttons, tag people (as discussed earlier), edit the photo's individual caption and other options, delete the photo, or designate the photo as your current profile picture.

Photo Comments

Photos are the ultimate conversation starters, so every photo you post gets its own individual comments thread. Down at the bottom of the page you'll see the field where viewers can enter their comments. Facebook will send you a notification each time someone adds a comment to one of your photos (or any photo you've been tagged in, even if it's part of someone else's collection).

Editing and Adding Photos to Existing Albums

Once you've created an album, you can go back to it anytime to edit its info, delete photos, or add photos (up to the limit of 60 per album). Go to the Photos application, and click the My Photos link. You'll see a listing of each of your albums, with the most recently updated albums at the top of the list.

| Share | + |

Tag This Photo
Edit This Photo
Delete This Photo
Make Profile Picture

The additional controls that appear at the bottom of the page for each individual photo

TIP: Once your album is ready for viewing, you can click the Share Album link at the bottom of the page to send an Inbox message to friends you'd like to come take a look at it. Facebook also gives you a Post to Profile link, but it isn't really necessary—your album will show up as a story on your Wall as soon as you've created it.

Public Images, Unlimited Down at the bottom of the page for each photo you upload, as well as for each album as a whole, Facebook gives you a public URL that can be accessed without signing in to Facebook. You can send this URL to anyone you'd like to see your photos who isn't a member of Facebook, and you can also use it to link to Facebook photos on blogs or other Web sites.

NOTE: You can delete an album by going to Photos > My Photos and clicking the Delete Album link for the album you want to get rid of.

Click the Edit Album link for the album you'd like to work with. You'll be taken to the same Edit Photos page you saw when you created the album, where you can change the captions and other options for each photo. To add photos, click the Add More tab, which will open the photo uploader. From there the process is the same as when you created the album.

Sharing Video on Facebook

TIP: The Video application is part of your Facebook account by default, but if the bookmark is missing for any reason, you can restore it using the Edit Settings dialog on the Applications page. If the Video app itself is missing from your authorized applications, you can restore it by searching.

Facebook's Video app does for video what Photos does for still images. Like its counterpart, Video gives you multiple easy ways to post original content to your profile. And once you've done that, Facebook provides you with a built-in audience thanks to its News Feeds and notifications, which ensure that your friends will see your work—and maybe your friends' friends, too, depending on the privacy settings you choose. (On the other hand, since each video you post gets its own specific Privacy control, if you want to post something just for family or a small group of friends, you can do that, too.)

And just like YouTube videos, Facebook videos can be embedded on blogs and other outside sites—making your potential audience as worldwide as the Web itself.

Viewing Videos

As with photos, Facebook gives you a variety of ways to see videos created by your friends, or videos in which your friends are tagged. Here are some of the key places to watch Facebook's never-ending video festival.

The Home Page

Although videos don't get their own tab on the Home page's News Feed like photos do, video stories do show up on the Posted Items tab, as well as on the main News Feed tab itself.

The Video Application

You can access the Video application via the bookmark in the Applications pop-up menu or the Applications area on the Home page.

The Home page for the Video app shows you the latest videos posted by your friends, as well as videos in which your friends have been tagged recently. Click on the thumbnail for any video to go its page, where you can watch the video and comment on it.

Viewing Videos by a Specific Friend

While you're in the Video app, you can see all the videos belonging to a specific friend by clicking the View *Name's* Videos link that appears next to each video. You can also go directly to a friend's profile and look for the Video box (if they've chosen to display it), or the View Videos of *Name* link under their profile button. (If the friend in question hasn't posted or been tagged in any videos, the link won't appear.)

Click the link under a friend's profile picture to see their videos.

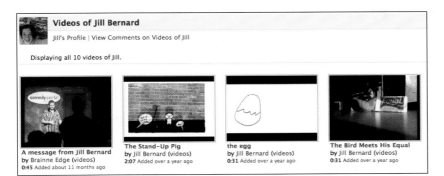

Posting Original Videos

Facebook gives you three convenient ways to post your original videos. From within the Video application (one of the basic Facebook apps that's part of your account by default), you can post an existing video file from your hard drive, record a new video from scratch using your Webcam or other video camera that's connected to your system, or upload a video from your mobile phone. (See the *Going Mobile* chapter for info on mobile uploads.)

Remember that videos you upload or record to Facebook need to be less than 20 minutes long, with a file size of less than 1024 MB. (If your account is new, Facebook may limit you to 2 minutes and 100 MB until you verify it. In that case, click the "Verify your account" link in the upload dialog for further instructions.) If your file exceeds those limits, Facebook won't let you upload it.

TIP: If you have longer videos or films already hosted on other sites, you don't necessarily need to duplicate that content on Facebook. Instead you might consider posting a short teaser or trailer to whet viewers' appetites, and then direct them to a URL where they can view the entire work.

Uploading a Video from Your Computer

In the Video application, click the Upload button, which will take you to the dialog where you can select a video.

🎥 Video My Videos | Videos of Me | About | Help   **+ Upload   ● Record**

NOTE: In order to emphasize that you should upload only original videos you've created yourself, Facebook stipulates that any videos you upload should be made by you or one of your friends, and should feature you or one of your friends.

Create a New Video

File Upload	Mobile Video	Record Video		Back to My Videos

Select a video file on your computer.

[   ] (Browse...)

Please upload a file only if:

- The video is under **1024 MB** and under **20 minutes**.
- The video was made by you or your friends.
- You or one of your friends appears in the video.

In the File Upload dialog, use the Browse button to navigate to the video file you'd like to upload. Facebook will begin uploading your file, and the Video Data form will appear where you can enter basic info about your video during the upload and after it's complete.

Enter the following info while you wait for your upload to finish.

Title: [Interview with Kiwi (A Brief Q&A)]

Description: [I conduct a brief question-and-answer session with my feline companion, Kiwi.]

Privacy: 🔒 Who can see this?
[Everyone ▾]

[Save Info]

Give your video a name and type a brief description, and then use the Privacy menu to choose who will be allowed to see the video.

When you're done entering the info, click the Save Info button to proceed to the page for your new video.

Recording a Video

To record a brand-new video using any video camera attached to your computer, go to the Video application and click the Record button in the upper right-hand corner, next to the Upload button.

The Record a Video tab opens, with the Adobe Flash Player Settings dialog displayed. Use the Camera menu to choose the camera you'd like to use, if it isn't already selected.

Click through the various other settings to make sure everything's ready to go, and then click the Close button to exit the Flash Player Settings.

If you haven't already granted Facebook access to your camera, you'll see the dialog below. Click the Allow button to proceed.

The Camera settings for Adobe Flash Player

Facebook will open the video recorder window—click the circle button to begin recording, and the same button (which changes to a square) to stop.

The Privacy settings for Adobe Flash Player

Left: The Record button. Right: The playback controls.

The Local Storage settings for Adobe Flash Player

You can play back your video to see how it turned out. If you don't like it, you can click Reset to delete it and start over. If it's good to go, you can click Save to proceed.

Once you click Save, you'll arrive at the Edit Video page, where you can tag people, assign a title and description, and set the Privacy controls. You can also click through various frames of the video to choose a thumbnail image that will represent the video when it appears on Facebook pages.

The Microphone settings for Adobe Flash Player

When you're all done setting these options, you can click Save to finish. You can also click Skip for Now to save the video without setting any options, or

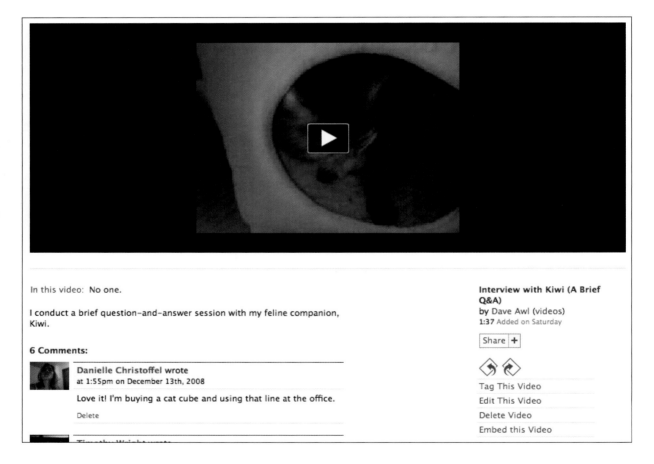

TIP: Just like photos, each video on Facebook has a public URL down at the bottom of its page, which can be accessed without signing in to Facebook.

Delete to erase the video. If you click Save or Skip for Now, you'll proceed to the page for your new video.

Additional Video Controls

Once you've uploaded or recorded your video, you'll arrive at the page for the video, where you'll see some additional controls. You can tag people who appear in the video, use the rotate buttons to change the video's orientation, edit it, delete it, or embed it somewhere else.

In this video: No one.

I conduct a brief question-and-answer session with my feline companion, Kiwi.

6 Comments:

Danielle Christoffel wrote
at 1:55pm on December 13th, 2008

Love it! I'm buying a cat cube and using that line at the office.

Delete

Interview with Kiwi (A Brief Q&A)
by Dave Awl (videos)
1:37 Added on Saturday

Share +

Tag This Video
Edit This Video
Delete Video
Embed this Video

Video Comments

Just like photos, each video you post gets its own comments thread, with a field down at the bottom of the page for viewers to enter their comments. Facebook will send you a notification each time someone posts a comment about one of your videos (or any video you've been tagged in).

Tagging Videos

Tagging videos works much like tagging photos. Click the Tag This Video link on the video's page, and type the names of the people you want to tag in the box. When you're finished, click Done Tagging.

Embedding Facebook Videos

As mentioned earlier, any video you've posted to Facebook using the Video application can be embedded on other sites, just like YouTube videos. On the video's page, click the "Embed this video" link. The "Embed your video" dialog will open, with the Embed code displayed.

From there, all you have to do is copy and paste the code. Click the Okay button to close the dialog once you've got what you need.

Adding a Video Box or Tab

If you haven't already done so, you can add a box for the Video application to your profile. You can also assign the Video app its own tab if you want to give your videos some extra prominence on your profile. Go to the Applications page, choose the Profile tab in the Edit Settings dialog for the Video app, and click the option to add a box, a tab, or both.

Using Photos and Videos Promotionally

One of the interesting things about both photos and videos is that while they're creative works in their own regard, they're also ideal media for showcasing *other* creative works. And when you factor in the way Facebook's News Feeds push photos and videos out to the people in your network—with the passive endorsement effect to increase their reach and impact—they become highly effective tools for promoting projects, events, and even ideas.

So in addition to posting funny pictures of your cat, your kids, or your most recent trip to Mexico, it's worthwhile to think about how you can use Facebook photos and videos to tap into an audience for whatever else you use your talents to create.

If you're in a theater company with a show about to open, for example, you might post some shots of rehearsals in progress, headshots of the cast, or flyers and posters for the show itself. If you make handcrafted jewelry or furniture, post some samples of your work. If you bake, show everyone your latest cake; if you're a knitter, show off your latest scarf or sweater. You get the idea.

Facebook videos can be a great promotional tool, too. Conduct short interviews with your collaborators, or have a friend interview you about your latest project, event, or cause. You can use Facebook to video blog, or to get your message out through short films, sketches, or original songs.

This is not meant to encourage anyone to blatantly spam Facebook's News Feeds, by the way: To be effective, you need to make sure that what you post is genuinely engaging and appealing to your Facebook friends. If it feels too much like crass advertising, instead of enlarging your audience you'll wind up alienating people and encouraging them to defriend you.

On the other hand, if you give people something compelling and worthwhile to look at, Facebook will help make sure they see it.

9

Group Dynamics

Most of the interactions covered so far in this book have been between people who already know each other. But there's a whole big Facebook world out there beyond your Friends list, and Facebook's Groups are the common areas—the cafés and clubs, if you will— where you can mix with people you don't know yet, and maybe get to be friends with them eventually.

Facebook's Groups are also useful for enabling communications among subsets of your Friends list, or tracking down old friends you haven't yet connected with on Facebook.

And because Facebook's Groups tap into the power of its social networks and News Feeds, they're an effective tool for spreading ideas and drawing attention to issues and causes.

In this chapter, we'll start by looking at the many ways to use Groups on Facebook. Then we'll talk about how to find and join Groups that interest you. And finally, we'll walk through the process of creating and managing new Groups of your own.

TIP: Facebook's Friend Finder (discussed earlier in the *Friends* chapter) lets you automatically search for members of your graduating class. But suppose you specifically want to track down members of your old marching band, including friends who were older or younger than you? One strategy is to create a Group for the band and then keep an eye on its members list. Some of the friends you're looking for may find their way to the Group before you find them individually on Facebook.

Facebook Groups Are Here All Week

Because the names of Facebook Groups ripple through its News Feeds, and everyone loves to pass on a good joke, Facebook Groups with amusing names have practically become their own genre of comedy.

Some Group names make sardonic comments about life (such as Disney Gave Me Unrealistic Expectations About Love), while others use the tried-and-true stand-up comic's technique of identifying something small but universal—like the Group called I Flip My Pillow Over to Get to the Cold Side. (On the other hand, a Group called I Tried To Smother My Roommate With A Pillow And Failed So Now It's Awkward has only attracted 837 members as of this writing—which should probably come as a relief to annoying roommates everywhere.)

Pop cultural references are fertile ground, too (The Finer Things Club is a joke only fans of *The Office* TV series will get), and hometown humor springs eternal—there are endless local variations of the You Know You're From Peoria When … motif. If your town isn't represented yet, maybe you can fill the void.

Groups: Free-Associating on Facebook

On the surface, the idea of Facebook Groups is simple. Facebookers with a common interest form an online club, with its own page where members can mingle and socialize. This provides a convenient way to meet new people outside your geographical area and real-world social scene. And Groups are an ideal forum for geeking out—they allow fans of someone or something to connect with their fellow devotees, sharing information, photos, videos, and general chitchat about the object of their obsession.

But there are other ways you can put Groups to work, above and beyond those obvious uses. Groups can help you track down old friends, for example. (See the tip at left.) They also make an excellent tool for communicating with collaborators on creative endeavors, as well as work groups and project teams. (In the example shown later in this chapter, I created a Group to help me keep track of the people who graciously gave me permission to use their names and faces in this book.)

Perhaps most importantly, joining a Group makes a statement. When you click the Join button, the Group's name and the fact that you've endorsed it are broadcast to your Wall and your friends' News Feeds (subject to your privacy settings). That makes Groups great tools for propagating memes and messages of all kinds.

Groups can be used to air a pet peeve—such as No, I Don't Care If I Die At 12 AM, I Refuse To Pass On Your Chain Letter, or the ever-popular Group called People Who Always Have to Spell Their Names for Other People (which, by attracting so many members, has proven that almost everyone feels that way). A Group dear to the hearts of copy editors, I Judge You When You Use Bad Grammar, is the *Eats, Shoots, and Leaves* of Facebook—with upwards of 300,000 members, it's been written up in the *New York Times* and the *Wall Street Journal*, and even spawned a spin-off book due out in 2009.

Groups can be used to make political statements as well as personal or pedantic ones. Myriad Groups supporting and opposing candidates raged through Facebook all during the 2008 presidential campaign. Facebook's Groups can be an effective tool for grassroots organizing, too, and for grabbing the attention of politicians and the media—Groups that attract thousands of members become de facto petitions, often generating news stories as their memberships climb. And because anyone on Facebook can create a Group, there's something fundamentally democratic about their use as a new way to give ordinary citizens a megaphone.

Joining Groups

Becoming a member of a Facebook Group is as easy as clicking a button or a link. No dues to pay, no loyalty oath to swear—you don't even have to wear a silly hat. Unless you want to.

Generally, you'll be doing the clicking in one of two places: either the Requests page, because you've been invited to join a Group, or the Home page for a Group you've found on your own.

Responding to Group Invitations

Invitations to join a Group work pretty much like the app requests discussed earlier in this book: They're flagged out in the Requests area of the Home page, and appear on the Requests page itself. You can click Confirm to join the Group or click Ignore to make the invitation go away without joining.

> **You have 6 group invitations.**
>
> **Knitting Keeps Me Sane**
> Common Interest - Hobbies & Crafts
>
> You have been invited by Kevin Spengel.
>
> Would you like to join this group?
>
> [Confirm] [Ignore]
>
> Ignore All Invites From This Friend

Joining a Group from Its Home Page

If you find your way to a Group you haven't been invited to, just look for the "Join this Group" link. It's usually located in the upper-right corner of the Group's page—right under the photo, if there is one.

> View Discussion Board
> Join this Group
> [Share] [+]

> Request to Join Group
> [Share] [+]

If the link says "Request to Join Group" (as in the shot on the right), that means it's a closed Group, and one of the Group's admins has to approve any new members before they're allowed to join.

TIP: If a friend keeps sending you invitations to Groups you're not interested in, you can click the Ignore All Invites From This Friend link underneath any Group invitation they've sent you. Future Group invitations from that friend will be automatically ignored.

Open, Closed, or Secret

In the real world, some clubs are open to the public and others are private. That's true of Facebook Groups, too, and they come in three degrees of exclusivity:

Open Groups are the most welcoming. Anyone can join an open Group and send invitations to others. The Group and its content are visible to everyone on the Network the Group belongs to.

Closed Groups are more exclusive. Only people who receive an invitation, or whose request to join is approved by an admin, are allowed to become members. Nonmembers can see basic group info, but only members can see content such as photos and discussions.

Secret Groups fly below the radar for maximum privacy. Groups designated as secret don't appear in the directory and can't be found by searching. The only way to find out about a secret Group is to get an invitation to join.

Groups are also limited to specific Networks—only people who belong to the designated Network will be able to see and join the Group. Groups on the Global Network can be seen by everyone on Facebook.

Finding Groups

Here are some of the ways you can find Groups to join on Facebook.

News Feeds

One of the best ways to find out about new Groups is to keep an eye on the News Feed on your Home page. You'll see stories appear occasionally telling you that a friend of yours has just joined a Group. If the Group looks interesting, you can click on its name to check it out, and then join it if you decide you want to.

> 👥 Kevin Spengel joined the group Knitting Keeps Me Sane. 11:11pm - Comment

Friends' Profiles

You may also notice interesting Groups in stories on your friends' Walls, or in the Groups listing on the Info tab of their profile.

Groups	See All (41)
Member of:	The Curious Theatre Branch, DOCTOR WHO, I want a TARDIS, Dave Awl Has Permission to Use My Name & Photo in His Book Facebook Me!, Southern Poverty Law Center, THE SONNETS, BigBridge, Theater Oobleck, Tracey Ullman fan club, Lawyers for the Creative Arts, Bradley Forensics Alumni Network, Roddy Frame and Aztec Camera Fans, Myopic Books Poetry Reading Series, Chicago, New York Neo-Futurists, Stephen Fry's

Searching for Groups

You can search for Groups using the search field in the blue bar, as well as within the Groups Application (see below).

The Groups Application

There's one other important way to find new Groups: the Groups application, which is both a directory of Groups on Facebook and a tool for managing and keeping track of the Groups you belong to. Groups is one of Facebook's basic applications, added to your account and bookmarked by default.

The left-hand column on the Home page for the Groups application shows you a listing of Groups that have been recently joined by your friends—which is a great way of keeping in touch with the trends and interests your social circle is embracing. The right-hand column shows you Groups you belong to that have been recently updated or changed, with the changes highlighted in yellow.

The pop-up menu on the My Groups page lets you display your Groups according to different criteria.

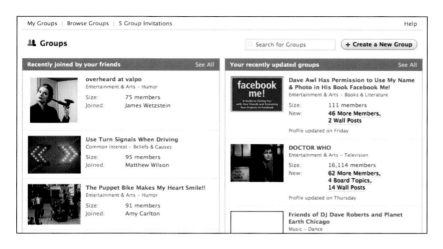

Clicking the My Groups link at the top takes you to a listing of all the Groups you currently belong to, with a pop-up menu that lets you sort by different criteria. Clicking the Browse Groups link takes you to a directory page that lets you browse for Groups by category and Network.

The filter menus on the Browse Groups page let you browse for Groups within Networks you belong to, and by type of Group.

Communicating in Groups

Once you've joined a Group or six, you may want to take the plunge and get to know the other members. Most Groups have two main ways for members to communicate with each other: the Wall and the discussion board.

Type		
Entertainment & Arts	▾	
Subtype		
All		
Books & Literature		
Celebrities		
Comics & Animation		
Dance		
Fashion		

Various subcategories appear depending on what you choose from the Type menu on the Browse Groups page.

The Wall

The Wall for a Group is a simplified version of the Wall on an individual profile: Members can post short comments, which appear in the order they were posted. Admins for the Group have the ability to delete inappropriate postings.

The Discussion Board

For slightly more organized conversations, the discussion board organizes comments by topic. Group members can create new topics, kicking off the conversation with a question or provocative comment, to which other members can respond.

Discussion Board

Displaying 3 of 10 discussion topics   Start New Topic | See All

Being An Account of The Life, Death, and Occasional Rebirth of An
Extremely Short Play.
4 posts by 1 person. Updated on August 26, 2008 at 9:04am

NOTE: Both the Wall and the discussion board are optional features, so some Groups you join may be missing one or both. In the latter case, the only way to communicate with your fellow members is by sending them Inbox messages.

TIP: By default, Facebook sends you a notification whenever someone replies to a post you make on a discussion board, so you can keep up with the conversation without having to obsessively check the board every ten minutes.

WARNING: Facebook explicitly forbids the creation of Groups that "attack a specific person or group of people (e.g., racist, sexist, or other hate groups)," and says that "creating such a group will result in the immediate termination of your Facebook account."

TIP: Before you start the process of creating a Group, be sure to read the "Group or Page?" sidebar on the facing page, to make sure a Group is what you really want.

You can click the See All link in the upper-right corner to view all the existing topics on a Group's discussion board, and use the pop-up menu to filter the list for topics you've created, or topics created by your friends.

Clicking Start a New Topic opens a simple form that asks you to name the topic and then kick it off with an initial post.

Posting Content

Depending on what the Group's creators and admins have chosen to allow, members may also be able to contribute to the Group by posting photos, videos, and Web links (aka Posted Items).

Creating Groups

Prior to creating a group, you might want to prep the materials you'll need ahead of time. You'll want to:

- Choose a photo or graphic to use on the Group's page.
- Write a brief description of the Group: its nature, purpose, and mission. Keep this to a short summary—just a couple of sentences. You can type a longer message in the Recent News area of your Group's page.
- Decide whether the Group will be open, closed, or secret.
- Decide whether the Group will be Global (open to all members of Facebook) or available only to members of certain Networks. For example, you might want a campus club to be visible only to members of your school's Network, or the Party Planning Committee for your workplace to be limited to your company's Network.

When you're ready to create your Group, start by going to the Groups application and then click the Create a New Group button at the top of the page.

Search for Groups   **+ Create a New Group**

Your recently updated groups   See All

Step 1: Group Info

Once you click the button, you'll arrive at the Step 1: Group Info page. This is where you enter the basic details about your new Group: its name, its description, and any recent news you'd like members (and prospective members) to see on its page.

From the Network menu, choose either Global or one of the Networks you belong to, as discussed earlier. From the Group Type menu, choose from the various categories to classify what kind of group it is. Fill in the optional contact info, such as e-mail and street addresses, and the city or town where your Group is headquartered, at the bottom of the form. When you're done entering your info, click the Create Group button to proceed.

WARNING: The one piece of info that you can't easily change after you leave this page is the name of the Group itself. Facebook is riddled with Groups that have typos and misspellings in their names, because by the time their creators discovered the mistakes, the Group already had dozens of members and the name of the Group was locked.

Facebook disallows name changes in order to prevent a certain kind of mischief: creating a Group with an innocent name, waiting till it attracts members, and then changing the name to something embarrassing or offensive—or simply a name that no longer accurately reflects the views of the people who signed on. After all, if you join a Group called "I Like Apples" one day, you shouldn't have to log in the next day and discover that overnight you've become a member of a group called "I Hate Oranges."

So before you click the Create Group button, take a minute to look over the name of the Group you're creating. Make sure it's exactly the name that you want. Reread it letter by letter to make sure there are no typos in it.

Group or Page?

Hold the phone just a minute. Before you go ahead and click the button to create a new Group, you might want to take a minute to ask yourself whether what you really want to create is a Facebook Page.

Pages, as mentioned earlier in this book, are used to represent public figures, organizations, and business entities that need to communicate with large numbers of fans, customers, or supporters. Bands, theater companies, nonprofit organizations, and small businesses (such as bookstores, restaurants, or nightclubs) are ideal candidates for Pages. For those users, Pages have a number of advantages over Groups—including the ability to send updates to an unlimited number of subscribers (whereas Group admins are limited to a maximum of 5000 members when sending messages).

If you're not sure which is appropriate for your needs, here's a good rule of thumb: Groups are best for *horizontal* communications, whereas Pages are best for *vertical* communications. If you want to enable conversations within a group of peers who share a common interest, create a Group. On the other hand, if you want to send one-way communications from a single public figure or organization to a large group of fans, you should create a Page. See the *Page and Ads* chapter for more info.

TIP: If you have an existing Group that you'd like to have converted into a Page, you can submit a request to Facebook. As long as your Group meets the appropriate criteria for a Page, Facebook will handle the conversion for you. See the *Pages and Ads* chapter for details on the requirements for Pages.

NOTE: Group photos are limited to a file size of 4 MB or smaller. If you try to upload a larger photo, Facebook will scold you and tell you to choose a smaller file. In that case, you might want to check the resolution for your image and make sure that it's 96 dpi or less—there's no need to use a higher-quality image than that.

TIP: You can bypass the options on the Step 2 page by clicking the Skip button at the bottom of the page, and come back to them later on.

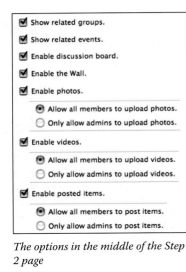

The options in the middle of the Step 2 page

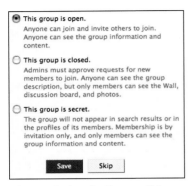

Choose whether the Group will be open, closed, or secret.

Step 2: Customize

Once your Group is created, your next stop is the Step 2: Customize page, where you can upload a picture and set some further options for your Group.

In the Upload Picture area, use the Browse button to navigate to the image on your hard drive that you'd like to use for the Group. Select the checkbox certifying that you have the right to use the picture and it doesn't violate Facebook's Terms of Use, and then click the Upload Picture button.

If there's an external Web site associated with the Group, you can enter it in the Website field.

Then use the checkboxes in the middle part of the dialog (see the images at left) to choose whether you'd like optional content to be displayed; specify who can post photos, videos, and posted items; and designate the Group as open, closed, or secret. When you're all done setting those options, click Save to proceed.

Facebook will ask you if you want a story to be created that will appear on your Wall announcing the new Group you've just created.

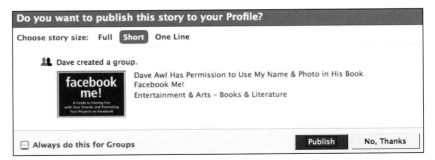

You can decide on the size of the story by clicking the Full, Short, or One Line button. Click on Publish to allow the story to appear, or No, Thanks to continue without creating the story. Once you exit the dialog, you'll be taken to the Step 3 page.

Step 3: Members

The final step of the Group creation process is to send out some invitations, using the Invite People form on the Step 3 page.

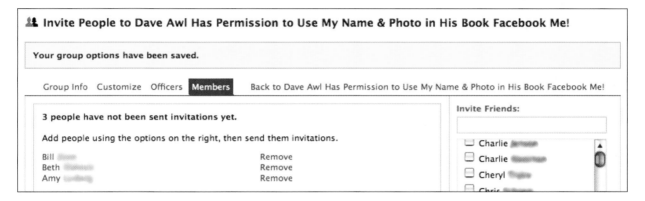

As you select the checkboxes on the right, names will be added to the list of people you're inviting on the left. (If you add someone by mistake or change your mind, you can click the Remove link next to their name to take them off the list.)

You can type a short greeting to your invitees in the Personal Message box—it always helps to add the human touch and tell people a little about why you're sending them this invitation.

TIP: You can also invite people who aren't members of Facebook yet to join the Group, using the "Invite People who are not on Facebook via Email" box on the Step 3 page (shown below).

When you're ready, click the Send Invitations button. Facebook will give you a confirmation message when the invitations have been sent.

You're now officially done creating your Group. To see the fruits of your labor, click the link in the upper-right corner that says "Back to *name of your Group*," which will take you to the Home page for your new Group.

You can quickly access the Groups for which you serve as admin using the pop-up menu on the My Groups page.

Message All Members
Edit Group
Edit Members
Edit Group Officers
Invite People to Join
Create Related Event
Leave Group

Share +

The links on the Home page for a Group as they appear to an admin. None of these are visible to ordinary members except Invite People to Join, Leave Group, and the Share button.

Officers

Dave Roberts
DJ
Dave Awl
Moderator
Danielle Christoffel
Webmaster

The list of Officers appears on the Home page for the Group.

Managing Groups

As creator or admin, you have the responsibility of keeping an eye on your Group to make sure it grows and thrives. Think of your role as similar to that of the host at a party: You want to make sure new arrivals feel welcome, help keep the conversation flowing, and serve as a buffer if arguments break out.

The quick and convenient way to access the Groups for which you're an admin is to go to the Groups application, click My Groups, and then select Groups You Admin from the pop-up menu.

You can always update or change the basic info for the Group that you entered when you created it—with the important exception of the name of the Group, as noted earlier. On the Home page for the Group, click the Edit Group link and then make changes as desired.

Promoting Members to Admin

Every Group starts out with one admin: the person who created it. But it's helpful to have more than one person to keep an eye on things, especially if it's a popular Group or one that's topical enough to provoke debate.

You can promote members of the Group to admin status by clicking the Edit Members link and then clicking Make Admin next to the name of the person you want to promote. People you promote to admin gain the ability to edit the Group's info, promote or remove members, create officers, delete Wall posts, delete discussion board topics and posts, and create related Events.

Richard Cooper (London)   Remove | Make Admin

Removing Members

To remove a member from the Group, click the Edit Members link and then click the Remove link next to the name of the person you want to eject.

Adding Officers

Officers for Groups are purely ceremonial figureheads—the position doesn't come with any special duties or privileges. But people you designate as officers for the Group are displayed in a list on the Group's page—and listing these prominent members can give the Group credibility, or help convey a sense of who its movers and shakers are. If your Group has formal officers such as a president, vice president, treasurer, and so forth, this is the place to list them. On the other hand, if you want to anoint key members with whimsical titles drawn from the works of Dr. Seuss, feel free.

To add or edit officers for your Group, click the Edit Group Officers link on the Group's Home page. Click the Make Officer link next to the name of each person you'd like to designate. Enter a title for each person in the Make Officer dialog that appears, and click the Make Officer button to confirm. Your updated list of officers will appear on the Group's Home page. You can return to the Edit Group Officers page anytime to add or remove officers.

Sending a Message to Your Group

You can use the Message All Members link on the page for your Group to send an Inbox message to everyone in the Group's member list. (However, this option is limited to Groups that have fewer than 5,000 members.) The Message All Members link is visible only to admins.

Moderating Posts and Discussions

As admin, you have special powers you can use for good—to help keep your Group's discussions on-topic and spam-free, and to squelch flame wars and other unpleasant distractions. You can delete any Wall comment that's inappropriate by clicking the Delete link for that post. For discussion boards, you have the option to mark posts as irrelevant in addition to deleting them. Marking a post as irrelevant hides the post but doesn't remove it: Members can still view a hidden post by clicking the Show Post link next to it.

Creating Related Events

Clicking the Create Related Event link on the Home page for your Group lets you set up a calendar item that's linked to your Group. The name of your Group will appear as the host of the Event, and the Event itself will appear in the Related Events box on the Group's page. See the *Facebook Calendar* chapter for more info on creating Events.

Moderating in Moderation

If you're used to moderating groups on other services, such as Yahoo Groups or Google Groups, you'll find that the moderation options for Facebook Groups are somewhat limited in comparison.

Although you can delete individual postings, or hide them (using the "Mark as Irrelevant" feature), there's no way to set a Facebook Group so that all posts must be approved by a moderator before they appear, and you can't assign different levels of posting privileges to different members of the Group. That means moderation of Facebook Groups is an after-the-fact activity, and you may need to keep a fairly close eye on your Group's Wall and discussion board if you want to keep the conversation on-topic and in bounds.

Everything's a trade-off, of course. Despite the limited moderation controls, creating Groups on Facebook pays off by allowing you to take advantage of Facebook's News Feeds and Networks to draw attention to your Group and help it grow.

The links that appear next to each post on a discussion board. The options to reply directly to the person who made the post, or to report the post to Facebook, appear to all members. The options to mark the post as irrelevant or delete the post are visible only to admins.

10

The Facebook Calendar

Call it "the social butterfly effect": Social networking sites have triggered a pleasant metamorphosis in the process of organizing social events. In the old days—not so long ago—keeping track of the invitations and RSVPs for a large gathering could be a real headache for the host. And as a guest, you often had no idea whether there'd be lots of groovy people you knew at a particular event, or whether the high point of your evening would be something wrapped in phyllo dough you snagged from a passing hors d'oeuvres tray.

But over the last several years, sites like Evite have made it easy for hosts to manage guest lists online and for attendees to see who else is planning to show up. Facebook ups the ante even further by connecting event invitations to its Networks and News Feeds, making it easy to spread the word and assemble a crowd for public events like performances, benefits, grand openings, or club nights.

All of which means that one social butterfly flapping its wings—or rather, clicking its mouse—can cause a fabulous party to erupt just a few days later. And you can find out about it just by clicking your own mouse on Facebook's Events app.

In this chapter, I'll show you how to use Facebook's Events application to find upcoming Events in your social network, as well as how to create and promote your own. We'll also look at how Facebook helps you keep track of your friends' birthdays, and some of the fun ways you can use Facebook to send birthday greetings. And while we're on the subject of calendars, I'll cover a few third-party calendar apps you can choose to install.

The Events Application

When in the course of Facebook events it becomes necessary to invite your friends to a swell soiree, let your fans know about your band's next gig, or drum up a crowd for any other kind of get-together—well, that's when the Events app comes in mighty handy. The Events app (which is one of Facebook's basic applications) also serves as a resource for finding out about fun things to do when you're planning your own social itinerary—it's a little like a hip friend who knows where all the best parties, concerts, gallery openings, and poetry readings are. All you have to do is ask it.

TIP: After an Event is over, it doesn't disappear in a puff of smoke—you can visit its page the next day, or even weeks later, to post photos and videos from the event itself and talk about what a hoot it was with the other attendees. The Past Events tab in the Events app is one easy way to get there.

The Home page for the Events app has four tabs. Upcoming Events shows you Events you've been invited to that are happening in the near future. Friends' Events shows you Events your friends are planning to attend, so that you can scope out what's on their social radar. Past Events is an archive of Events you were invited to that have already taken place. (This comes in handy for remembering what you did last weekend—especially if you had such a good time that it's all a blur.) The Birthdays tab shows you friends with birthdays coming up soon. (More about that toward the end of this chapter.)

Profile of an Event

Each Event that's created on Facebook gets its own page. Much like a Group's page, the page for an Event has (at the option of the Event's creator) its own Wall, as well as areas for photos, videos, and links related to the Event.

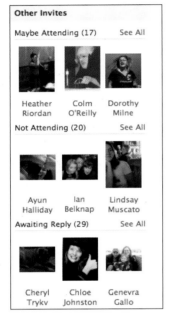

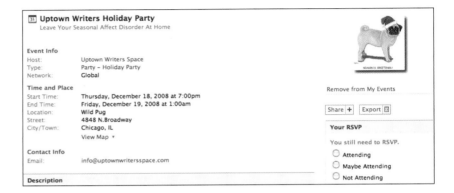

The Other Invites box on the page for an Event shows the Maybes, the Noes, and the ones who haven't answered yet.

The Confirmed Guests box shows you people who have RSVP'd "Yes" to this Event, so you can see who's currently planning on showing up. Along the right side of the Event page, you can see the other invitees—those who aren't coming, those who said "Maybe," and those who haven't replied yet.

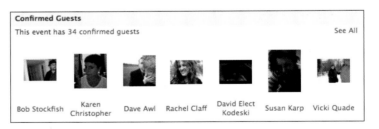

Responding to Event Invitations

Invitations to Events show up as Event requests, which appear on the Requests page and are flagged out in the Events and Birthdays area on the Home page. An Event request works pretty much like an app request or a Group request. Click Yes to tell the host you'll be there with bells on; click Maybe if you'd like to go but you're not so sure about the bells just yet. Click No to tender your regrets.

If you want to find out more about the Event before you RSVP, just click on the name of the Event to go check out its page.

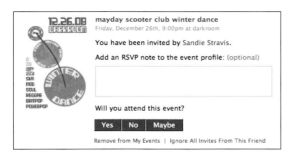

Once you respond, you'll show up in the appropriate category on the page for the Event: Confirmed Guests, Maybe Attending, or Not Attending. The Event request will disappear from your Requests page, but the Event itself can still be viewed on the Events Home page, and a reminder will appear on your Home page a few days before the Event takes place.

Keeping Track of Events

As mentioned earlier, you can always check the Upcoming Events tab in the Home page to see what's going on in the near future. But in case you're not that proactive, don't worry—Facebook has you covered.

The Events and Birthdays Area

For starters, as long as you check in on your Home page on a regular basis, you'll see reminders for your upcoming Events appear in the Events and Birthdays area in the right-hand column. Events show up in this area three days before they take place and then disappear the following day.

Events that appear on your Home page include (1) any Event you've confirmed your attendance for, and (2) any Event you've been invited to but haven't responded "No" to, or removed from your Events.

Exporting Events

You can also export your Facebook Events as an ICS (iCalendar) file, which can be imported into many calendar applications such as Microsoft Outlook, Apple iCal, Google Calendar, and more.

To export all your Events, go to the Events app and click the Export Events link at the top of the page. To export any specific Event, go to its page and click the Export button, which is right next to the Share button in the right-hand column.

Events and Birthdays   See All
Today, December 23 at 8:30pm
Hope! Hope! Hope! A Rock Show Benefitting Chicago Coalition for the Homeless
Friday, December 26 at 9:00pm
mayday scooter club winter dance
Tomorrow
Genevra Gallo
Friday
Bryn Magnus

The Events and Birthdays area of the Home page. Clicking the See All link takes you into the Events application—so it's really just a shortcut to the app.

Share + Export

The Export button lives right next to the Share button on the page for an Event.

TIP: Before you start creating your Event, you might want to prep a few items ahead of time, so that you have them handy as you're working:

1. A photo or graphic for your Event page
2. The basic facts: time, date, address, and contact info
3. A short description of the Event that will appear in the Description area of the page.

WARNING: As with Groups, the name of an Event can't be changed once it has confirmed guests. So before you click the Create Event button, be sure to proofread the name of the Event carefully to make sure it doesn't have any typos or misspellings.

Open, Closed, or Secret

Like Groups, Events come in three types: open, closed, or secret.

Open Events allow anyone to add themselves to the guest list, whether or not they've been invited, and send invitations to their friends. Anyone on the Event's selected Network can see its info, Wall, and photos, as well as News Feed stories about the Event.

Closed Events require an invitation in order to RSVP, and only admins can send invitations. The Wall and photos are visible only to invited guests. However, anyone on the Event's Network can see its basic info and send a request for an invitation to the admins. News Feed stories about the Event won't be visible to anyone who hasn't been invited.

Secret Events can't be found by searching, and none of the Event's info or News Feed stories will be visible to people who haven't been invited. Like closed Events, they're invitation only, and only admins can send invitations.

Creating an Event

Ready to create a Facebook Event? Go to the Events app and click the "Create an Event" button at the top of the page. You'll arrive at the Step 1: Event Info page, where you enter the basic data about your Event.

Type the name for your Event—make it snappy and succinct. You don't need to include the date or the place in the name itself, because you'll be entering that farther down. In the Tagline field you can enter a punchy phrase that will appear below the name of the Event—something to convey a sense of what it's all about, or just communicate the mood and personality of the Event.

From the Network menu, choose Global if you'd like the Event to be visible to everyone on Facebook, or limit it to a specific Network if you prefer. Use the Event Type menus to select a category and subcategory. Type the Event's description in the field provided, and use the menus to enter the start and end times for the Event. In the bottom part of the dialog, you can add the location, address, and optional contact info, and then click the Create Event button to proceed to the next step.

On the Step 2: Customize page, use the Upload Picture area to browse for a photo or graphic on your hard drive. Then set the options below: Decide whether guests are allowed to bring others or if this is an "invitation-only" event. Decide whether you'd like a Wall to appear on the Event's page or not; whether to allow photos, videos, and posted items to appear on the page;

and whether guests are allowed to upload those things, or only admins. In the bottom part of the page, specify whether the Event should be open, closed, or secret. And finally, choose whether or not you want to publicize this Event by allowing it to appear in search results. Once you've set all those options, click Save to proceed.

Now it's time to let some people know about your Event. On the Step 3: Guest List page, use the checkboxes to choose friends (or Friend Lists) you'd like to send invitations to.

Step 1: Event Info	Step 2: Customize	Step 3: Guest List		Finish and View

Show: Attending   ▾

Showing 1 out of 1 guests

Dave Awl (Chicago, IL)   Remove

Invite Friends:

☐ Becca Freed
☐ Becky Morgan
☐ Beth Delaich

You can use the Personal Message field to type a short greeting to the people you're inviting. And you can use the "Invite People who are not on Facebook via Email" box to send invitations to your non-Facebook friends.

Add people using the options on the right, then send them invitations.

Trent A. Creswell   Remove

Personal Message (optional)

Send Invitations

Invite People who are not on Facebook via Email:
Enter emails separated by commas

Import email addresses from your Yahoo, Hotmail, AOL, Gmail or MSN address book.

Add

Left: the Personal Message field. Right: the box for inviting nonmembers of Facebook.

Once you're done sending invitations, click the Finish and View button at the top of the page to look at the page for your Event.

📅 **Edward appears on "Check Please"**
Finally, a reality show that will have him.

Event Info
Type: Music/Arts – Performance
Network: Chicago, IL

Time and Place
Date: Friday, November 21, 2008
Time: 8:00pm – 8:30pm
Location: Your television (Channel 11 in particular)
City/Town: Chicago, IL

Remove from My Events

Don't be afraid to think creatively about what constitutes an "event"—it doesn't necessarily have to involve people getting together in the same location, for example. My friend Edward created a Facebook Event to let friends know about his appearance on Check, Please!, *a TV show on which customers review local restaurants.*

TIP: Don't feel obligated to disclose an e-mail address or phone number while you're creating the Event if you don't want to. This is Facebook, after all, so anyone who wants to get in touch with you can send you an Inbox message (unless you've changed your privacy settings to disallow that).

Creating Related Events
If the Event you're creating will be hosted by a person or organization who has a Group or a Page on Facebook, you can create it as a Related Event (assuming you have admin privileges for the Group or Page). This means that the Event will show up in the Events area of the Group or Page that it's related to, and the Group or Page will be listed as the Host for the Event on the Event page.

To create a Related Event for a Group, go to the Group's page and click the Create Related Event link.

To create a Related Event for a Page, go to the Page, find the Events box, and click "Create Events" or "Edit."

NOTE: If you're creating a Related Event for a Page, you'll get an optional extra step in the process. The Update Fans page will appear as Step 3, giving you the opportunity send an update message to all the fans who have subscribed to your Page. If you're not ready to do that now, don't worry—you can come back and do it later. (See the *Pages and Ads* chapter for info on updates and how they work.) In this workflow, the Invite Friends page will appear as Step 4 instead of Step 3.

TIP: On the finished page for your Event, you'll see a View Map link listed under the location, which links to a Google Map of the address you supplied.

Party Out of Bounds

"Who's to blame when parties really get out of hand?" the B-52's wondered back at the dawn of the '80s. Lately there have been a number of news stories blaming Facebook for that phenomenon—such as the horror story in the UK press about a family whose home was trampled by 300 gatecrashers who turned up at their daughter's 16th birthday party. According to news accounts, the birthday girl had originally sent the invite to 100 friends on Facebook.

Of course, Facebook isn't the only medium used to spread the word about parties online—MySpace, e-mail, mobile phones, and instant messaging play a role, too. Still, in the age of rapid-messaging technology, before you advertise any event online you should ask yourself how you'll handle things if the crowd that turns out is bigger than expected.

If you choose to promote your event in public, make sure the venue can accommodate the number of people you're inviting and their guests. Set contingency plans in place in case the crowd exceeds expectations—make sure you have people you can trust to cover the door if necessary, and turn away guests who can't be accommodated once the venue is at capacity.

And as those news stories underscore, you should be *very* cautious about publicly promoting parties on Facebook that take place in someone's home. Consider setting the Event as secret, or at least closed, and avoid posting your home address in the invitation itself. Remember that you can always send that info to the invited guests separately, as an Inbox message.

Promoting Your Event on Facebook

If the Event you've just created is open to the public and you're hoping for a large turnout, there are a number of ways to promote it on Facebook. Of course, the first and most important step is to send out invitations—not only to let the people you're inviting know about the Event, but also because each time one of them clicks Yes, a News Feed story may be generated that tells their friends about the Event, thus expanding your audience.

And ultimately, that's the key to promoting your Event on Facebook—getting its name to appear in Facebook's News Feeds as often as possible (without overdoing it in a way that annoys your friends).

Here are some other good strategies:

- When you create your Event, make sure the name is snappy and engaging. The name is all your invitees will see in the invitation itself, so you want it to get their attention and convey the Event's appeal. Try to inject a little humor if possible.
- When you send out your invitations, I highly recommend using the Personal Message field to include a short greeting. This will help you grab your invitees' attention and increase the odds that they'll respond (or at least check out the Event's page).
- Mention the Event in your status update.
- Write a Note about the Event.
- Post the Event to your profile using the Share button on the page for the Event. Remember that when you post something to your profile, the story also appears in the Posted Items tab of your friends' News Feeds (as well as the Live Feed and possibly the main News Feed tab as well). If there's a long lead time of several weeks, you can probably even get away with doing this once a week or so without seeming too pushy.
- Post photos, videos, and links on your Event's page, and start a conversation on the Wall for your Event. News Feed stories get generated each time people comment on your Event's photos, videos, and posted items, as well as when they post on your Event's Wall—and each of those stories will contain the name of your Event and a link to its page. When someone else comments on something that's part of your Event's page, make it a point to answer or thank them with a comment of your own—thus keeping the conversation going.

You'll be most effective if you space these actions out in time, so that they don't seem like overkill—or desperation.

Finally, if you decide you'd like to advertise your Event on Facebook, it's easy to do. On the Invitations page (which you can access by clicking the Invite People link on the Event's page) you'll find a link that says "Promote Your Event with an Ad." Clicking that link will take you through the process of creating a Facebook Ad. See the *Pages and Ads* chapter for more info about Facebook Ads.

Managing an Event

Once your Event has been created, you can manage its guest list and various options from the Event page itself. In the list of links that appear underneath the photo, you can cancel the Event if necessary, invite more guests, edit the Event's info, print a list of attendees, and send an Inbox message to all of the guests. (If the Event is hosted by a Page, instead of an Inbox message you can send an update to the Page's fans.)

If you'd like some help with your hosting duties, you can add admins to an Event by clicking the Edit Guest List link on the Event's page, and then clicking Make Admin next to the name of the person you'd like to promote.

> Invite People to Come
> Cancel this Event
> Edit Event
> Message All Guests
> Print Guest List
> Remove from My Events

The admin links on the page for an Event. Visitors who aren't admins won't see most of these.

Birthdays on Facebook: The Year-Round Birthday Party

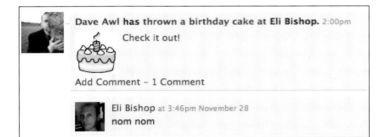

If you ask me (and since you're reading this book, I suppose you did), one of the most fun aspects of life on Facebook is that it's almost always someone's birthday. After all, it's always satisfying to let your friends know how much they mean to you when their birthdays roll around, and Facebook gives you a number of easy ways to do that.

But let's face it: The older you get and the more friends you acquire, the harder it gets to keep all those dates rattling around in your cranium. Fortunately, with Facebook on your side, you no longer have to—all you have to do is keep an eye on the Events and Birthdays area of your Home page, and Facebook will tip you off several days in advance of your friends' birthdays.

When your own birthday arrives, you can expect your Wall to fill up with greetings from your friends—even the ones who don't normally remember your birthday—thanks to the fact that Facebook has tipped them off. And the rest of the year, you get to be the one who remembers all of your friends'

TIP: If you're really into birthdays and don't always check the Events and Birthdays area of your Home page, you can also choose to get reminders from Facebook via e-mail when one of your friends has a birthday on the horizon. Go to Settings > Account Settings > Notifications to edit your e-mail notifications. Under the first category, Facebook, click the Show More link to reveal the hidden options, and then select the "Has a birthday coming up" checkbox.

Something from the YouTube Gift Shop?

If you want to post a greeting that's a little more animated than just writing "Happy birthday" on your friend's Wall, searching up a YouTube video to post in their honor makes for a fun Facebook-style gift.

Start by identifying someone or something you know your friend is a fan of: a band, a TV show, a comedian, a cartoon character. (Scanning the Info tab on their profile might give you a clue if you're drawing a blank.) Then go to YouTube and type the relevant name in the search field, along with the word *birthday*. Very often you'll turn up something fun and surprising. You can then use the Share Link button above the Publisher on your friend's profile to post the video to their Wall.

For example, my friend Herman is a devoted Smiths fan. So for his birthday I typed *Morrissey* and *birthday* into YouTube's search field and found a live video of the crowd singing "Happy Birthday" to Morrissey at one of his concerts. Typing *birthday* and *Doctor Who* into the search field turned up a fan-made video of a Dalek singing "Happy Birthday," which was perfect for my friend Steve, a fellow Whovian. (He didn't even mind being threatened with extermination before the toy Dalek self-destructed ...)

The profile box for the Birthday Calendar application

special days. Of course, not everyone chooses to make their birthday public on Facebook, so most likely you'll have some friends who won't show up in Facebook's Birthday notifications. But for those who do, here are a few fun ways to give them a shout-out:

1. Write a message on their Wall. This is the simplest and most direct option. Creativity is always appreciated—but on the other hand, if you can't think of anything clever, there's nothing wrong with a simple "Happy Birthday."

2. Send a gift, using any of the gift apps discussed in the *Communicating on Facebook* chapter.

3. Use SuperPoke to "throw a birthday cake at" your friend. (See the *Communicating on Facebook* chapter for more about SuperPoke.) Other apps have birthday features you can take advantage of, as well.

4. Post a video. Dedicate a song or a find a video you know will make your friend laugh. (See the sidebar "Something from the YouTube Gift Shop?")

Other Calendar Applications

In addition to the Events app, there are several third-party applications that can help you with calendar and scheduling functions. Here are three of the most popular (all of which you can find in the Applications Directory):

- **Birthday Calendar**, as you might guess from the name, is focused on birthdays. It lets you put a box on your profile that displays a list of upcoming friends' birthdays along with their profile pics. Inside the app you can view all of your Facebook friends' birthdays laid out in a printable calendar-page format, month by month for the coming year. A selection of electronic greeting cards and gifts is built right into the app.

- **SocialCalendar** also creates a graphic calendar display, and in addition to birthdays it lets you track anniversaries, get-togethers, and other social occasions. It also lets you post and compare wish lists to make present shopping easier. An activity feed within the app lets you keep an eye on what events your friends are adding to their own calendars.

- **Weekly Schedule** lets you put a box on your profile that displays a graphic schedule of your activities, so your friends can see at a glance when you might be free to get together. Within the app you can automatically compare your schedule with those of your friends. My pal Shaina says this is one of the best apps on Facebook for college students who are trying to keep track of each other's complicated class and work schedules.

11

Pages and Ads

Welcome to the chapter on Pages—and please notice the capital *P*. There are thousands of pages on Facebook, but only some of them are Pages.

As I've mentioned a few times in earlier chapters, a Facebook Page is a special kind of profile that allows public figures, organizations, and businesses to communicate easily with throngs of fans, supporters, or customers. Pages (which Facebook also refers to as *public profiles*) offer valuable demographic information and traffic statistics to let Page administrators (*admins* for short) know what kinds of visitors have been checking out their Pages and what those visitors are interested in.

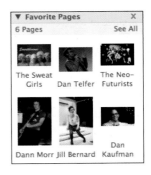

There are other advantages to Pages, too, which we'll address in the course of this chapter. First we'll look at how you can find Pages for people and organizations you admire, and subscribe to them for updates. Then I'll take you through the process of creating, managing, and promoting Pages of your own.

At the end of the chapter, we'll talk about how to take advantage of Facebook's paid advertising options, if you've got the budget and the inclination. And finally, we'll take a brief look at the Marketplace application—Facebook's answer to classified advertising.

Facebook Pages 101

Pages vs. Groups and Profiles
Pages are one of the most under-utilized tools on Facebook, which is why I've been mentioning them constantly throughout this book. Often, people who want to set up a presence for a band, a comedy group, or even a bookstore create a Group (or in some cases a personal profile) when what would really serve their needs best is a Page.

One reason for this confusion is that people who are more familiar with MySpace expect Facebook to work similarly. On MySpace, people create profiles to represent all kinds of entities, and fans create MySpace profiles in honor of bands or other public figures they're not personally affiliated with. But as mentioned in earlier chapters, on Facebook the rules are different. Profiles represent individual people, whereas organizations are best represented by Pages (or in some cases, Groups). And nobody is allowed to create a profile for a person other than themselves, or a Page for an entity they don't officially represent.

Another reason is that everybody has the Groups app installed by default, and the button for creating a Group is right there in plain sight when you go into the Groups application. By contrast, the controls for creating a Page are hidden away under the Advertising link down in Facebook's footer.

As discussed in the *Group Dynamics* chapter, however, there are a few circumstances where Groups may suit your needs better than Pages: for example, if you're looking to create a gathering place for fans of a public figure, but you aren't an authorized representative of that public figure. (See the sidebar "Fake Pages: Swim at Your Own Risk.")

On the surface, Facebook Pages look a lot like the pages for Groups and Events. There's a place for an identifying image or graphic up top; space to provide basic info and facts; boxes for photos, videos, and related Events. Fans can interact with each other using the Wall and discussion board.

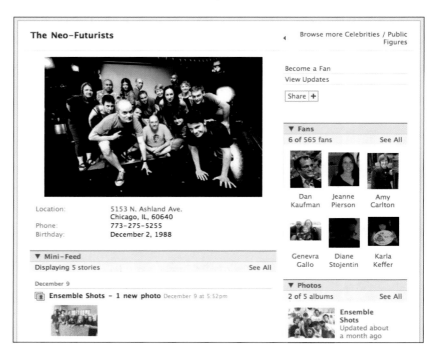

But Pages offer a number of special advantages for the people who maintain them:

- With Pages, you can send updates to an unlimited number of fans or supporters. (By contrast, admins for Groups can send messages only to a maximum of 5,000 members.)

- Admins for Pages don't have to approve friend requests. When people choose to become a fan of your Page, they're automatically approved—which can be a real time-saver if your Page attracts hundreds or even thousands of fans.

- Pages can be customized with apps. Groups can't.

- Admins have access to statistics on the traffic and activity for their Page.

Becoming a Fan: Finding and Subscribing to Facebook Pages

If you keep an eye on the News Feed and your friends' profiles, you'll see stories about Pages popping up regularly—telling you that a certain friend has just "become a fan of" a band, film, TV show, local restaurant, or charity organization. (If the Page is for a political figure, the story will say "became a supporter" instead of "became a fan.")

You can click on the name of the Page in the story to go check it out, and become a fan or supporter yourself if you choose. But you don't necessarily have to wait around for a News Feed story to tip you off. If you're wondering whether there's a Facebook Page for someone or something you admire, you can search for it using the blue bar's search field.

Once you find your way to a Page you'd like to become a fan of, all you have to do is click the link that says "Become a Fan" in the upper-right area of the Page. Becoming a fan of a Page does three things: First, it generates a News Feed story, as shown above. Second, it adds the Page to the Pages area of your Info tab:

Pages   See All (53)

> Mad Men
> TV Show

> Kids in the Hall – Live As We'll Ever Be!
> Comedian

> Crowded House
> Musician

> Farm Sanctuary
> Non-Profit

And third, it subscribes you to updates from the Page. (See the "Checking Your Updates" section.)

 TIP: Breaking up with a Page is easy. If you decide you no longer want to be a fan or supporter, just go to the Page and click the "Remove me from Fans" link.

TIP: Clicking the "Browse more *Name of Category*" link in the upper-right corner of a Page takes you into the Pages directory, where you can browse for other Pages by category and also check out what Pages your friends have become fans of recently.

NOTE: When you become a fan of a Page, the creator and admins for the Page don't gain access to your e-mail or other contact info, so your privacy is protected.

The orange flag icon next to a search result indicates that it's a Page.

Become a Fan
View Updates

The Become a Fan link

NOTE: Facebook limits the number of Pages you can become a fan or supporter of to 500. That's a pretty generous limit, but if you have a compulsive fangeek personality like me, you might want to restrain yourself a little so that you don't hit the ceiling some day. A good rule of thumb might be to click the Become a Fan link only when you feel real passion for, or a personal connection to, the Page in question—rather than just clicking it for anything you recognize and like.

Checking Your Updates

Once you've become a fan or supporter of a Page, you'll be subscribed to its updates, which are messages sent by the creator of the Page or its other admins. If the Page is for a band, you may get updates about upcoming concerts or album releases. Pages for TV shows might send updates about the new season or DVD releases, while updates from politicians' Pages are likely to focus on campaigns, political issues, or fundraising. You get the idea.

When you have new updates to read from any of the Pages you've subscribed to, you'll see them flagged out in the right-hand column of your Home page.

> **Updates**
> 🖵 2 new updates

Clicking one of those notices takes you to the Updates page (which is also accessible by clicking the Updates tab in your Inbox). On the Updates page, you'll see all your recent updates in chronological order.

The column along the right shows you the various Pages you're subscribed to: Clicking a name will show you just the updates for that specific Page.

Opting Out of Updates

If you'd like to stop receiving updates from a Page you're subscribed to—without removing yourself from its fans—you can click the Opt Out link underneath any update from that Page. You can click the Edit Update Settings link (at the bottom of the right-hand column on the Updates page) to see the Update settings for all of the pages you're subscribed to, and disable or re-enable updates for any of them.

Fake Pages: Swim at Your Own Risk

In theory, Facebook forbids the creation of Pages by anyone who isn't an authorized representative of the entity that the Page represents. Facebook is about real identities, after all, so the policy for Pages is consistent with the policy for personal profiles: no impersonations, aliases, or pseudonyms allowed.

In practice, however, Facebook's directory is crowded with Pages that were created by fans eager to have a place on Facebook for their favorite writer, musician, or artist.

Complicating matters, it isn't always easy to tell an authentic Page from a fake one—although one dead giveaway (pun intended) is if the Page is for a long-departed writer like Shakespeare or Emily Dickinson.

(Well, that's assuming the writer in question hasn't been authorizing the Page and dictating updates via Ouija board.)

If you choose to create such a Page, or become a fan of one, be aware that Facebook may choose to invoke the rules and deactivate the Page (and the accounts of its creators) at any time—especially if Facebook has any reason to believe that the admins for the Page are using it to deliberately impersonate someone else.

Your best option, if you want to express your love for a public figure or organization who doesn't have a Page yet, is to create a Group where you and your fellow fans can geek out together in a nondeceptive, peer-to-peer kind of way.

Creating a Page

To begin the process of building your brand-new Page on Facebook, start by clicking the Advertising link in the footer, down at the bottom of any Facebook page. When you get to the Facebook Advertising page, click the Pages tab at the top.

You'll arrive at a page with information about Pages and how they work, which you can click through if you want to. When you're ready, click the Create a Page button to begin.

TIP: Before you start creating your Page, you might want to prep a few items ahead of time, so that you have them handy:

1. The name for your Page.
2. A primary photo or graphic to illustrate your Page.
3. Info: Look at other Pages in the same category as the one you'll be setting up to see what kind of information you'll need.
4. Content: You might want to prepare some pictures and video clips to post on your Page, if applicable. If the Page is for a band, you might want to prepare some songs to upload to the Music Player, and information on releases for the Discography app.

Facebook Pages

Create a presence to engage your customers and let them engage with each other.

Create a Page

or manage your existing Pages

Step 1: Choose a Category and Name Your Page

On the Create a New Facebook Page page, your first task is to decide what category your Page belongs in. Choose one of the three top-level categories:

Setting Up a Business Account

If you're only on Facebook for work reasons—to set up a Facebook Page or other advertising on behalf of your employer or client—you don't necessarily have to set up a personal profile. You can set up a kind of limited account called a *business account* instead.

Business accounts don't have profile pages, aren't visible in search results, and can't send or receive friend requests. You also won't be able to view other users' profiles using a business account.

Note that you can create a business account only if you don't already have a personal account on Facebook.

To create a business account, first you'll need to begin the process of setting up the Page or ad that you're on Facebook to administer. You can do this by clicking the Advertising link on your Facebook Home page, which is visible without logging in. Once you've entered the basic info for your Page or ad, you'll be offered the option to create your business account and instructions on how to proceed.

Finally, if at some point you decide you'd like to convert your business account into a regular user account with a profile, you can do so by clicking the Create Your Profile button that's visible when you log in to your business account.

WARNING: As with Groups and Events, the name of a Page can't be changed once the Page has attracted some fans. So proofread it carefully and make sure it's correct before you click the Create Page button.

Local (for businesses such as restaurants, hotels, and cafés); Brand or Product; or Artist, Band, or Public Figure. Selecting one of those buttons will cause a pop-up menu to appear with a variety of more specific subcategories to choose from.

Once you've chosen a category, down at the bottom of the Page there's a field where you'll enter the name of your Page.

Naming Your Page

Names for fan-based Groups on Facebook are often long declarative statements, such as *Lloyd Cole Is My Guru*, or *The Puppet Bike Makes My Heart Smile!!* Constructions like *Friends of DJ Dave Roberts and Planet Earth Chicago*, or *Tracey Ullman Fan Club*, or *An Appreciation Society for Edward John Moreton Drax Plunkett: Lord Dunsany*, are common, too.

Pages are different in this regard. The name for a Page should be the simple, unadorned name of the entity it represents. So if you're setting up the official Facebook Page for the B-52's, for example, you want the name of the Page to be simply *the B-52's*, rather than *Fans of the B-52's* or *The Facebook Love Shack and Wig Emporium of the B-52's*.

Think of it in terms of the News Feed story that will be generated when someone becomes a fan. You'll want that story to say "Dave Awl became a fan of the B-52's," rather than "Dave Awl became a fan of Fans of the B-52's," which is clunky and a tad Escheresque.

What's in a Category?

You also can't change the category for a Page once it's created, so choose carefully. If you decide later on that you want a different category, the only option is to delete the Page and re-create it using the new category—and of course, you'll lose any current fans in the process and have to start from scratch. (For this reason, you should take a look at the Page before you click the Publish button, and if you need to delete it and start over, do it before the Page has been publicized.)

This does matter, because different categories of Pages are set up with different informational fields and apps by default. A Page for a restaurant, for example, has fields for information that diners may be looking for, such as customer attire, parking availability, payment options, price range, and culinary specialties. A Page for a film offers fields for the director, cast, and screenwriter as well as a plot synopsis. A Page for a politician lists party affiliation, as well as the offices the politician currently holds and is campaigning for.

Your best bet is to do a little comparative category shopping before you create your Page—take a look at some Pages that fall into specific categories and choose the type that best suits your needs.

Admittedly, Facebook's selection of categories for Pages is less than complete—or satisfying. There are Film and TV Show categories for example, but no Book category. (There is a Writer category, but if a writer wants to create a separate Page for a specific book, they're stuck using a general category like Product or Other Public Figure.) There's also no specific category for theater companies—Other Public Figure is the best bet at present (although I know of one Chicago performance group that chose to classify itself as a "religious organization," apparently hoping to inspire religious fervor among its fans).

At this point, although your Page has been "created," it hasn't been published yet—meaning it's not visible to anyone else. Publishing your Page comes a little later in the process. For now, you're working on it behind the scenes.

Step 2: Upload a Photo

Once your Page has been created, you'll arrive at a blank template for your Page (shown on the following page) where you can start adding basic content and info. Your first step should be to add a photo or graphic to illustrate your Page. Choose something eye-catching and appealing that conveys the essence of the person or entity that your Page will represent.

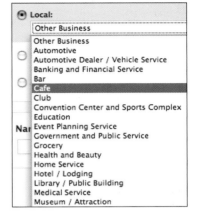

Some of the Local categories

The Brand or Product categories

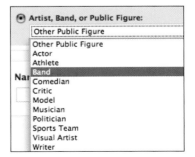

The Artist, Band, or Public Figure categories

Click the "Upload a picture" link under the yellow placeholder to open the Upload Picture tab, and use the Browse button to navigate to an image on your hard drive.

Select the checkbox to confirm that the image is yours to distribute and doesn't violate Facebook's Terms of Use. Then click Upload Picture.

Once your picture is uploaded, you can use the Thumbnail Version area to adjust how the mini version of the photo will appear. Facebook may use this thumbnail image to represent the Page in News Feed stories and other places around the site.

Step 3: Add Information

Next, you can add information to your page by clicking through the tabs for Basic Info, Detailed Info, and Contact Info.

The informational fields available will vary depending on the category you chose for your Page earlier. Fill out as much info as you'd like, and then click the Save Changes button for each tab. When you're done with these tabs, click the "Back to editing *Name of Your Page*" link to continue.

Step 4: Add Content

Next you'll arrive at the Edit Page page, which gives you all the links for editing and adding content to your Page, in one central place. From this page (which contains many more controls than are shown below) you can add photos and videos, create Related Events, write Notes, and more.

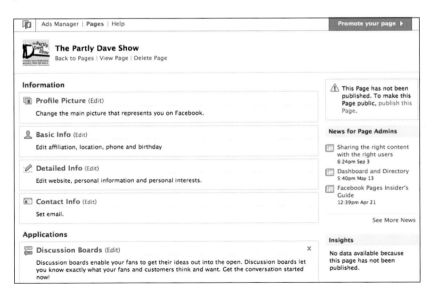

The Page Manager
In the process of creating and editing your Page, you'll be working in Facebook's Page Manager app. Because Page Manager is built by Facebook, it's automatically authorized when you need it—you won't see an "Allow" dialog like you do for third-party apps. You can add or remove a bookmark for the Page Manager app, if needed, from the Applications page.

If you have content ready to go, you might want to add some of it now, so it's there on your Page when you publish it. But you can always come back to this page to add content later on, so there's no rush. Once you're ready to move on, you can take a look at your Page to see how it's shaping up by clicking the View Page link (even before it's published) at the top of the page.

Edit Page
Edit Admins
Send an Update to Fans
Promote Page with an Ad
Add to my Page's Favorites
Remove me from Fans
Remove from my Page's Favorites
View Insights

The admin links on a published Page

Step 5: Publish Your Page

Notice the message across the top of your Page, telling you that it hasn't been published yet. At this point, your Page should be ready to greet its public—so you can go ahead and publish it by clicking the "publish this Page" link. (You can also publish the Page using the similar link on the Edit Page page.)

⚠ This Page has not been published. To make this Page public, publish this Page.

Managing a Page

Once your Page is created, you can accomplish most of its care and feeding using the Admin links on the Page itself. Using those handy shortcuts, you can edit the page's info, add other admins for the Page, send updates to your Page's fans, view Insights for your Page, and more.

You also have some control over layout: The boxes on your Page can be rearranged by dragging them, just like the boxes on a Profile page. Move the boxes you want your visitors to see first to the top of the Page to give them prominence, and move less important ones to the bottom.

Adding Admins to Your Page

If you'd like to give admin privileges to others so that they can help you manage the Page, click the Edit Admins link on your Page. The Edit Admins page uses an interface similar to the controls for inviting people to Groups or Events. Use the checkboxes to select the people you'd like to promote to admin, and they'll be sent an invitation. Once they accept it, they'll appear in the list of admins.

Restricting Access to Your Page by Age or Country

If you'd like to limit who can access your Page, you can do that on the Edit Page page. Scroll down to the Settings area, and click the word *Settings* to reveal the controls (shown on the facing page).

To set the minimum age required to visit your Page, use the Age Restrictions pop-up menu. (For example, if your Page is for a bar, you might choose the "Legal drinking age" option.) To set the countries from which people can visit your Page, click "edit" next to the words *Country restrictions*. Then use the checkboxes that appear to set which countries are allowed to access your Page.

*The controls in the
Settings area of the
Edit Page page*

*The checkboxes that appear under
the "Country restrictions" heading
when you click the "edit" link*

Setting a Gender for Your Page

You can also choose how your Page is referred to in News Feed stories. Use the Gender pop-up menu in the Settings area of the Edit Page page to choose the correct pronoun for your Page. For example, if your page is for a female writer, you'd want stories to use the pronoun *her* ("Dorothy Parker updated her profile"); for a band you'd probably want *their* ("The B-52's updated their profile"); and for a movie, TV show, company, or product you'd probably want *its* ("Arrested Development updated its profile").

Adding Applications to a Page

One of the advantages of a Facebook Page, as compared with Groups, is that you can add applications to Pages. In fact, some kinds of Pages come with apps pre-installed: A Page in the Musician category, for example, comes with a music player and the Discography app, which is designed to display a listing of all the recordings the artist has released so far.

To add an app to your page, go to the Page for the app (which you can find by searching or by browsing the Applications directory). Not all apps can be added to Pages, but if an app is Page-friendly, you'll see this on its Page:

You can add this application to some of your Facebook Pages.

+] Add to Page

When you click the button, you'll see a dialog asking you to confirm that you want to add the app to your Page. (If you manage more than one Page, you'll see a menu to select which Page you're adding the app to). Click the button to confirm.

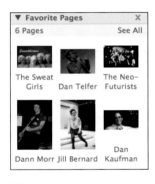

The Favorite Pages Box

The Favorite Pages box (shown above) lets you display a selection of other Facebook Pages you like. You can use it to give a sense of your Page's identity, showing off who you like and who you're allied with. You can use it to recommend other artists, causes, or products you think your fans would be interested in. And you can use it as a kind of link-exchange back-scratching tool: Adding someone else's Page to your Page may inspire them to return the favor, thus potentially sharing your fan base with each other.

To add a Favorite Page to your Page, go to the Page you want to add and click the "Add to my Page's Favorites" link in the upper-right area.

TIP: You can remove an app from your Page by clicking the X in the upper-right corner of the box for the app.

Promoting Your Page

The key strategies for promoting a Page are very similar to the tips for promoting an Event discussed in the previous chapter. The key is content, content, content: Customize your Page with timely info as well as photos, videos, music, and appropriate apps to make it a destination your fans want to come back to. Encourage conversations on your Wall, discussion board, and photo comment threads to keep generating News Feed stories. And of course, use regular updates to stay in touch with your fans.

You can also choose to promote your Page with a Facebook ad as discussed in the following section.

If you've got a Web site or blog, you can link directly to your Facebook Page. Facebook Pages are visible to all visitors, even the ones who don't have Facebook accounts or aren't logged in. (However, logging in to Facebook is required to post comments or view more than basic info on the Page.)

Fresh Data to Go

The chart shown at right is just a portion of the data available on the Insights page—you can track everything from page views to the number of new fans your Page attracts each day, as well as a demographic breakdown of your fans by age and gender. This is useful for gauging the effectiveness of content added to your Page, advertising, promotions, and other activity.

As a bonus, the data on your Insights page can be exported by clicking the Export Data link above the graph. You can choose to export the data as either an Excel (XLS) or comma-separated (CSV) file.

Sending Updates to Fans

One of the best ways to keep your fans coming back to your Page, and to stay on their radar, is to send out regular updates. Click the Send an Update to Fans link on your Page to open the form—which looks a lot like the form for composing an Inbox message. The one visible difference is that if you select the "Target this update" checkbox, you'll reveal the controls that let you send the update to specific subgroups of fans, selected by age, gender, or location.

Viewing Insights for Your Page

One of the great advantages of setting up a Page is that Facebook gives you access to a robust set of data regarding your Page's traffic, so you can see how much attention it's attracting, and how effectively the content you're posting is engaging your fans and other visitors. To access this data, click the View Insights link on your Page (which is visible only to admins).

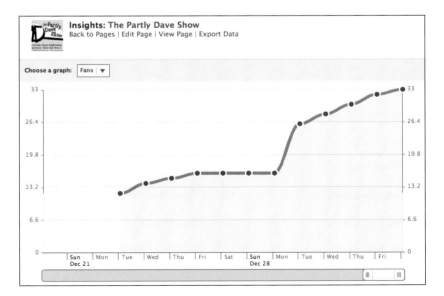

Facebook Ads and Social Ads

If you decide to invest some advertising dollars on Facebook, there are two options you can choose from: regular Facebook ads and Social Ads. Both kinds of ads let you supply your own art and copy and choose the users you'd like to target based on factors like age, location, gender, and keywords found in their profiles—helping your ad to find its way to the Facebook members who are most likely to be interested in it.

But there's an extra dimension to Social Ads: the passive endorsement factor. Social Ads let the viewer know when a friend of theirs has endorsed the subject of the ad—by becoming a fan of a Facebook Page, for example.

For both kinds of ads, you can choose to pay for advertising on a per-click or per-impression basis. Facebook lets you specify how much you're willing to pay for each click or impression, and set a daily maximum amount to spend. At the end, when your ad is prepped and ready to go, you'll need to enter a valid credit card number for the billing process.

Once your ad is live, Facebook will provide you with regularly updated stats to show you how your ad is doing and which categories of Facebook users are clicking on it the most.

To learn more and begin the process, click the Advertising link in Facebook's footer. You'll find a step-by-step guide to planning and preparing your ad, with lots of guidance on what's allowed and what will be most effective in reaching your audience.

An example of a Social Ad, which points out the fact that my friend Ellen has become a fan of the sponsor's Facebook Page.

TIP: If you've created a Page, Group, or Event, Facebook makes it easy to promote it with an ad. Pages have an admin link that says "Promote Page with an Ad" (example below). Groups and Events have similar links on their invitation pages. Clicking any of those links takes you to the page where you can start creating an ad.

Facebook Advertising

Reach your exact audience and connect real customers to your business.

Create an Ad

or manage your existing ads

| About Advertising | Prepare | Step By Step |

3. Reach the exact audience you want

Location: United States
● Everywhere ○ By State
Sex: ☐ Male ☐ Female
Age: 18 - Any
Keywords:

Female	Male		Age
			13–17
			18–24
			25–34
			35–44
			45+

Connect with Real People

- Reach over 130 million active Facebook users.
- Attach social actions about your business to your ads.
- Create demand for your product with relevant ads.

Create Your Facebook Ad

- Quickly create image and text-based ads.
- Precisely target by age, gender, location, and more.
- Choose to pay per click (CPC) or impression (CPM).

Optimize Your Ads

- Track your progress with real-time reporting.
- Gain insight about who's clicking on your ad.
- Make modifications to maximize your results.

Facebook Marketplace

You can think of Facebook's Marketplace application as its online classified ads section—or maybe the Facebook answer to Craigslist. Using Marketplace, you can create and browse listings for jobs, housing, vehicles, pets, services, and items for sale.

The advantage of using Marketplace, as compared with Craigslist or a newspaper, is that you can buy from, sell to, or connect with someone who belongs to your social network—a trusted friend, or a friend of a friend—instead of dealing with complete strangers. If you've got a great pair of concert tickets you can't use, for example, you might be happier knowing that your friends will get first crack at them. And if you're buying or selling a piece of furniture, you might be more comfortable arranging to meet someone with whom you share mutual friends.

As this book was going to press, Facebook was planning to launch a new, revamped version of the Marketplace application in February 2009. The screen shot below is an advance conception of what the new Marketplace is expected to look like. See Facebook's Help section for more info on Marketplace and how it works.

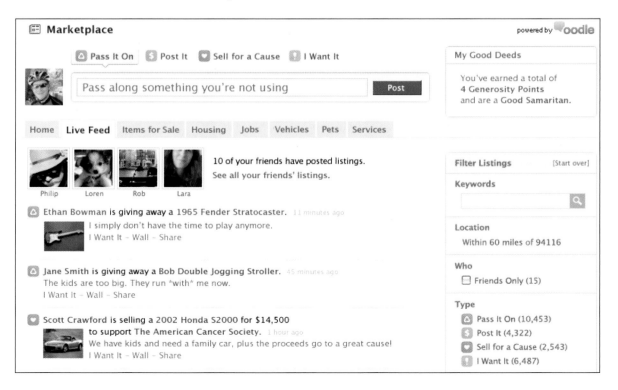

12

Facebook at Work

Finding a healthy relationship between work and one's personal life can be a tricky business, to put it mildly. So it's not surprising that the interface between Facebook and the nine-to-five world can be puzzling, too. Facebook is a fun, freewheeling, social kind of space, and work is, well—work.

So this chapter is about how to negotiate the boundaries between those two worlds. We'll start by tackling the ever-popular question of whether you should mix your social network with your work life, and whether it's even possible to keep them separate. Then we'll look at how Facebook can affect a job search in positive ways as well as negative ones.

And finally, I'll give you a few tips for staying in touch with your Facebook network even when you're working in settings where access to Facebook is blocked.

Should You Friend Your Boss?
Facebook and Office Politics

In the media stories I read about Facebook, there's one head-scratcher that pops up again and again: Should you be Facebook friends with your boss?

Ah, life was so much less complicated in the old days, before social networking meant anything other than business cards at cocktail parties. Darrin Stephens never had to worry about Larry Tate poking around in his Facebook profile, reading bad jokes from Uncle Arthur and naughty comments from Serena.

Add to this the fact that everyone's work situation is different. Different career paths, industries, and workstyles with differing professional standards lead to diverse relationships with varying boss personality types. (And if you're self-employed like me, or in the corner suite at your company, you can simply substitute the word *client(s)* for *boss* throughout this essay.)

And yet, to this complicated modern question I'm going to give you a very simple answer: Yes. Yes, you should be Facebook friends with your boss.

Because even if your boss doesn't know Facebook from a hole in the nearest putting green, you should be behaving as if he or she already *is* in your Friends list. People who aren't on Facebook today have a way of suddenly showing up when you least expect it. It may take three months, or six months, but when you factor in Facebook's current rate of growth—especially among older people—the odds are pretty decent that sooner or later you'll see a friend request from your boss pop up on your screen.

And if and when that day arrives, it's hard to imagine a boss–employee relationship where clicking Ignore would be the smart or politic choice. Which means that if your profile isn't already boss-friendly, you'll be frantically scrambling to clean up your Wall, photos, privacy settings, and so forth before clicking that Accept button. So why not get a jump on it?

The wisest course of action is to consider the professional standards that apply to your career—or the career you hope to have one day—and then apply them to your Facebook profile, now and going forward. If you keep your profile free of potential embarrassments as you go, then if the Facebook toothpaste does get out of the tube at some future date, you won't wind up with it smeared all over your résumé.

In some cases this may mean doing a little back-channel communication with your friends, via Inbox messages or other private means. If you have a friend who loves to post off-color jokes on your Wall, or photos you hoped were burned shortly after you graduated from college, it may help to proactively explain why you keep deleting and detagging what they post, and that it's nothing personal. (Well, unless it is.)

This line of thinking also applies to the related question of friending co-workers and colleagues. You may try to draw a thin beige line between your cubicle mates and your after-hours life—but if and when you start receiving friend requests from your co-workers, rejecting them could wind up lowering the temperature around the water cooler and in the meeting room. So it might save you some awkwardness in the long run to assume that your Facebook profile is an open book, and conduct yourself accordingly.

Ultimately, you don't have to suck all the fun out of your Facebook life in order to make it career-friendly—just think of your profile as an extension of the same persona you already use to socialize with people in your profession. And if you have a wild and crazy alter ego that's only for your non-work pals to see, you can still express it using Facebook's private channels, such as Inbox messages and one-on-one chats.

Facebook and Job Hunting

Facebook has the potential to be both a help and a hindrance when you're looking for work. On the plus side is, well, the networking part of *social networking*. Facebook makes it easy to get the word out about your work search to your entire social network. You can use your status update to let your friends know you're looking—ask them to keep their eyes and ears open for you, and let you know if they've got any appropriate leads.

Facebook's public conversations can be useful, too. If you pay attention to your friends' Walls, status updates, and comment threads, someone might mention an opening at their company, remind you of a mutual colleague you should get in touch with, or provide other useful leads.

Facebook Groups are a good resource: You may be able to find Groups related to your profession, where you can make new connections and net-work with people who work in your field but are outside your social circle.

On the minus side? Well, as discussed in the *Privacy and Security* chapter, lots of companies scour the Facebook profiles of job candidates, looking for reasons to chuck them in the bad apple bin.

According to a survey of hiring managers conducted by CareerBuilder.com, the most common dealbreakers they found on Facebook profiles included references to drinking or using drugs; "provocative or inappropriate" photos; poor communication skills, including bad grammar and spelling; lying about qualifications; and derogatory remarks about race, gender, or religion.

Fortunately, it's a two-way street: The managers also said that Facebook profiles could work in candidates' favor if they demonstrated that a prospective employee was intelligent, articulate, and professional, with solid communication skills and a wide range of interests.

Many are also speculating that the time will soon draw to a close when an embarrassing photo or two can kill someone's job prospects. Younger people increasingly live their lives in the open online, and as the working population ages, it's going to get harder for employers to find employees who have perfectly blemish-free Internet lives.

Back in the '90s, there was a much-discussed moment in corporate culture when companies decided to start hiring the "tattooed and pierced." Hiring managers realized that limiting themselves to candidates with conventional appearances had backfired, by screening out some of the most talented and creative prospects. By the same token, smart managers will eventually figure out that blackballing anyone with a questionable photo in their past could leave their company stranded in the shallow end of the talent pool.

Checking Facebook—Without Actually Checking Facebook

It's a shame that Facebook is viewed with distrust by some workplaces—especially since, as previously noted, Facebook can be a useful communication tool for work groups and project teams, a great way to get input and answers to questions, and of course an excellent forum for networking. Nonetheless, some companies see it as nothing but a time-waster and a drain on productivity, and block access to Facebook on their office networks.

If you find yourself working at a company where Facebook is blocked, you're probably not completely out of luck—because there are a number of ways to keep in touch with what's happening on Facebook without actually visiting the site.

E-Mail Notifications

As explained in the *Signing Up and Setting Up Your Profile* chapter, by default Facebook sends notifications to your primary e-mail address whenever someone writes on your Wall or sends you an Inbox message, among other actions. These e-mail notifications contain the full text of the messages they notify you about, so you can keep up with what your friends are saying to you just by checking your e-mail throughout the day. See the "Changing Notification Settings" section for more info.

RSS Feeds

As discussed in the *Wall, Status, and News Feeds* chapter, you can subscribe to a number of different kinds of feeds from Facebook—including your notifications, as well as your friends' status updates, Posted Items, and Notes. You can view these feeds using your Web browser, or an RSS reader such as Google Reader or Bloglines.

TIP: In addition to the other methods on this page, you can access Facebook using most current mobile phones. In fact, that's what the next chapter, *Going Mobile*, is all about.

The Facebook Toolbar for Firefox

This one won't help you if the Facebook site is completely blocked. However, it can be useful in a situation where Facebook is accessible, but having a Facebook window open on your screen all day might create, shall we say, the wrong appearance. With the toolbar installed (as covered in the *Applications and Other Add-Ons* chapter), you'll be notified whenever anything important happens—such as a new Wall post or Inbox message. That should help you keep your visits to Facebook short and to the point during working hours.

13

Going Mobile

Have I mentioned yet that Facebook can be kind of addictive? Even when you're out and about, away from your computer, you may sometimes find yourself with the urge to check in with your friends, update your status, or upload a photo—especially if you just saw something interesting on Mulberry Street.

Fortunately, you can take a big chunk of the Facebook experience with you in your pocket. Armed with a reasonably up-to-date mobile phone and nothing else up your sleeve, you can update your status, read and write Wall posts and Inbox messages, check your invitations, respond to friend requests, upload photos and videos, and more.

This comes in especially handy if you're stuck on public transportation, languishing in a doctor's waiting room, or trapped in any other zone of enforced boredom.

Exactly what you can and can't do on Facebook with your phone depends on its specific level of functionality. In this chapter we'll run through the various options, from the more primitive

(Facebook via text message) to the more sophisticated (Facebook via mobile Web browser, and Facebook apps for smartphones).

The Facebook Mobile Application

For best results, you should start your mobile Facebook life while you're still sitting at your desk—by accessing the Facebook Mobile application on your computer. The Facebook Mobile app gives you a central portal for instructions, settings, and features related to using your mobile phone with Facebook. If you don't already have Facebook Mobile bookmarked, you can find it by searching for the words *Facebook Mobile* in the blue bar or the Application Directory.

TIP: In addition to its other functions, you can use the Facebook Mobile app to browse a selection of photos your friends have recently uploaded from their mobile phones.

Mobile Uploads	Phonebook	Account	Help

🔲 **Mobile**   (+ **Activate Facebook Mobile**)

Facebook by Text Message

The simplest and most no-frills way to access Facebook by mobile phone is via text message. If your phone is capable of sending and receiving SMS text messages, and uses one of several supported carriers, you can access a slew of basic Facebook features just by texting.

NOTE: Facebook itself doesn't charge you anything for sending and receiving messages from your phone—but your carrier's standard rates will apply.

To get started, you'll need to activate Facebook Mobile on your computer. Go to the Facebook Mobile app and scroll down to the Activate Facebook Mobile area at the bottom of the screen (or use the Activate Facebook Mobile button at the top to jump down there).

Activate Facebook Mobile

You can update your status or look up profile information by sending a text to FBOOK (32665). You can also receive Facebook messages, Wall posts, and notifications sent to your phone as text messages. To get started, we'll text a confirmation code to your phone. (Standard text message rates apply.) Learn more.

Phone Number: Carrier:

| 17734122599 | AT&T ▾ |

e.g., 1xxxyyyzzzz
or 44xxxyyyzzzz

Activate

Already have a confirmation code?

*Facebook Mobile Texts are currently available only in US/Canada/UK on the listed carrier networks.

🖼 **Mobile Uploads**

Upload photos and videos straight to Facebook from your phone. Send an MMS to:

mobile@facebook.com

Confirmation code:

| | **Confirm** |

Mobile Web

Browse Facebook from your phone's internet browser. Go to:

m.facebook.com

Learn more about Mobile Web

US (1)
  AT&T
  Boost
  Cingular
  Helio
  Nextel
  Sprint
  Verizon
  Virgin USA
Canada (1)
  Bell Mobility
  Fido
  MTS
  Rogers
  SaskTel
  Solo Mobile
  TELUS
  Virgin Mobile Canada
UK (44)
  O2

The supported carriers menu in the Facebook Mobile app

NOTE: At present, accessing Facebook by mobile text messages is supported only in the United States, Canada, and the United Kingdom.

Facebook Text Commands
So what exactly can you do with Facebook Mobile text commands? Well, just for starters, you can update your status, write on someone's Wall, send an Inbox message, poke someone, or post a Note. For a complete list, including the necessary commands for each action, visit the Mobile Texts Demo page—where you can see a helpful onscreen demonstration of what each command does. You'll find it at www.facebook.com/mobile/?texts.

You'll need to enter your mobile phone number and then select your service provider from the menu of supported carriers. (If your service provider isn't listed, this method won't work for you, so you'll need to look at the other options in this chapter.)

Facebook will text a confirmation code back to your phone. (There could be a delay of up to an hour or so during busy times.) Once you get the code, go back to the Facebook Mobile app on your computer, click "Already have a confirmation code?" and enter your code in the field that appears.

See the sidebar "Facebook Text Commands" for more info about what you can do via text message and where to find a list of commands.

Facebook via Mobile Web Browser

If your phone is equipped with a Web browser, Facebook has a version of its site that's optimized for the smaller browsers found on handheld devices. The URL for the mobile site is http://m.facebook.com. (You can also type that address into your computer's Web browser for a preview of what the mobile site looks like.)

facebook
Home • Profile • Friends • Inbox (1)
Your status has been updated.
You have 6 friend requests.
You have 2 event invitations.
Create a Security Question.
We use security question to help identify you as the owner of your Facebook account if you ever need to write us for help.
You were poked by Roger Andreas Mueller. (poke back | remove)
Status Updates
Dave is finishing up Chapter 14 ... if it doesn't finish him first. (2 seconds ago) - Comment
Dave
[Update Status] [Clear]

If you're using an iPhone, you can navigate to http://iphone.facebook.com for an iPhone-specific version of the site.

TIP: Even if you point your phone's browser toward Facebook's regular URL, Facebook will most likely sniff out the fact that you're accessing it from a mobile device and redirect you toward the mobile version of the site.

Facebook Apps for Smartphones

There are special mobile phone apps available for a number of popular smartphones—including Facebook for iPhone, Facebook for BlackBerry, and Facebook for Palm. You can download these apps to your phone for a mobile Facebook interface that's custom designed for your specific device.

Facebook® for BlackBerry® smartphones
By Research In Motion, Ltd.
Facebook® for BlackBerry® smartphones provides automatic, wireless access to Facebook services – status updates, photo uploads, messaging, pokes and event invitations – for free!
2,769,132 monthly active users — 249 reviews

The listing in Facebook's Application Directory for the Facebook for BlackBerry app.

You can learn more about these apps by searching for them in Facebook's Application Directory—or in the case of the iPhone, the App Store.

Uploading Photos and Videos from Mobile Phones

You can upload content—specifically photos, videos, and Notes—to Facebook from any phone that's capable of sending multimedia (MMS) messages to an e-mail address and is (optimally) using one of Facebook's supported carriers.

To get started, send a photo or video from your phone as an MMS message to *mobile@facebook.com*—or send a Note to *notes@facebook.com*. If your phone hasn't previously been confirmed, Facebook will send you back a confirmation code to enter on the site (on the Mobile Uploads tab of the Facebook Mobile application). Once you've done that, you'll be able to upload freely, using those same e-mail addresses.

NOTE: If you're not using one of Facebook's supported carriers, Facebook says that you "should" still be able to upload photos and videos—but it's not guaranteed.

TIP: Before you can upload videos to Facebook, you need to make sure you've added the Video application to your account. See the *Photos and Videos* chapter for details.

TIP: When uploading a photo, whatever you type for the subject line of your message will be the photo's caption on Facebook. When uploading a video, the subject line will become the video's title, and anything you type in the body of the message will appear as the video's description. When uploading a Note, the subject line of your message will become the title of the Note.

Index